How to Sell Yourself in an Interview

A Guide for the Non-Salesperson

Les Fenyves

Contents

Introduction

"You have to sell yourself in an interview!"

You hear this directive all the time from people who are willing to give you free interviewing advice. However, the statement is virtually never followed up with instructions on exactly how you should be doing the selling. The purpose of this guide is to fill this gap by giving you concrete, specific actions that you can take to sell yourself.

It is not the intent of this guide to turn you into a professional salesperson. Instead, it is meant to introduce you to only those basic selling skills that will be the most helpful to you and have the greatest positive impact as you interview for the next step in your career. So, don't become stressed or discouraged if you don't think you could succeed in sales. You are not trying to become a salesperson. You just want to be better at selling yourself than others interviewing for the same position.

Before I get into the meat of the subject, let's pause and think about the implications of the advice to sell yourself. In my opinion, the statement implies that:

1. You have to *know your product thoroughly*, and you are the product.
2. You have to *prepare yourself for each interview* in exactly the same way as a salesperson would, which is:
   - You have to polish your interviewing skills.
   - You have to plan for each interview just as salespeople plan for sales calls.
3. You have to *think and act in the interview as a salesperson would*, that is:
   - You have to *control the interview* through the skilled use of questioning techniques. An interview is not simply an oral exam where you passively answer questions that test your knowledge.
   - You have to *close* before you leave; i.e., you need to ask for a commitment, or at a minimum, for feedback.

To implement the above points in your interviews, you will need to emulate what successful salespeople do, which is:

1. They close; i.e., they ask for a commitment.
2. They control the sales call.
3. They know their products inside and out.
4. They invest the time to polish their sales skills.

In this guide, I will introduce you to these topics, and I will break down the selling skills you will need in an interview into fundamental building blocks that anyone can understand and master.

This book is divided into two parts. Part 1 is devoted to teaching you those elements of selling that, I think, are what you need in order to be effective in your interviews. You should study this section in its entirety. Part 2 contains a number of self-contained chapters on various additional topics related to interviewing. Some of these are extensions of subjects covered in Part 1. Others address matters that come up frequently in interviews and often give people trouble. You can study, skim or ignore these chapters according to your interests and needs.

I would like to point out to you that the advice in this document is not some theoretical construct conceived in an ivory tower. Instead, it is a set of proven techniques developed and learned through many years of real-world experience.

During my nearly forty years as a search consultant, I personally arranged more than 20,000 interviews between my clients and candidates. Furthermore, my colleagues also set up tens of thousands of interviews. As a result, what I will be sharing in this guide is what they and I learned from this experience to be the most effective methods you can use to get the job you want – *even when you are not the best qualified candidate.* This last assertion is true because it is *always the best interviewee who gets the offer* (regardless of whether or not they have the strongest skills for the position). Therefore, if you study and put into practice my advice here, you will become an outstanding interviewee and gain a tremendous advantage as you compete for desirable jobs throughout your career.

The prospect of having to sell yourself may be uncomfortable or even intimidating to some of you. Don't let this apprehension deter you. The skills I will be presenting in this document can be learned by most intelligent people with normal social and communication skills, even if English is not their first language.

If you focus on implementing the advice contained in this guide and take the time to polish your interviews as I advise, you will interview better than 98% of your competition. Guaranteed!

Part 1

A Short Course on Selling

1. Closing

What is Closing?

Closing, in the context of this document, is defined as asking for a commitment or, at a minimum, immediate feedback from the interviewer while you are still in the interview.

I am putting this topic first in this guide because:

- If the only thing you change in your interviews is to add closing, while leaving everything else the same, you will see at least a 50% improvement in your interviewing success rate. So, this section contains by far the most valuable advice contained in this entire document.
- Virtually none of your competitors for a position will try to close in the interview. In fact, it is a rare person who even asks the interviewer for on-the-spot feedback. Therefore, you will have an immediate competitive advantage in getting the job.

Why Closing Is So Important

People get job offers even when they fail to close. However, if you are that rare person who does close at the end of each interview, you will gain a great advantage because, by closing, you can:

1. Lock down the job offer

As the interview progresses, the interviewer gathers facts and impressions about you. They process these and turn them into opinions; e.g.,

- Fact: you answered the skills questions correctly.
  Opinion: you are competent to do the job.
- Impression: you came across as flat and unenthusiastic because you didn't feel well.
  Opinion: you do not want the job.

Ultimately, the interviewer will combine the facts, impressions and opinions to formulate a decision – yes or no. Virtually no one scores 100% in an interview, so the outcome of every interview can go either way.

Let's suppose that you score a combined 90% positive result in an interview. 90% is a high score. You would think that you would get an offer in this situation, wouldn't you? Yes, but only if you close by asking the interviewer to articulate a positive decision *while you are still in the interview*. If you walk out of the interview without a decision, things can go wrong for you; e.g.,

1. Interviewers are stressed and anxious about making a hiring mistake. As a result, the 10% negatives can start mushrooming in their minds and overwhelm the positives. Result: rejection.
2. A second candidate can come in who also scores 90% or even only 85% in the interview. The fresher candidate can easily displace you, or they flip a coin and you lose. Result: rejection.

The only way that you can guarantee that this does not happen to you is to close during the interview by having the interviewer articulate a positive decision in your favor *before* you leave the interview. In fact, this is the most important reason for closing – to capitalize on the interviews where you did well. You don't want such opportunities to slip through your fingers.

So, if at all possible, don't let the interviewer walk out of the interview with an *opinion*. Opinions are like freshly-poured concrete. They can easily be changed. Decisions, on the other hand, are like concrete that has already set. They are much harder to reverse. Therefore, do your best to make sure the interviewer walks out of the room with a *decision*, a decision to hire you! That way you can only lose out to a clearly superior candidate who also closes. That is extremely unlikely.

2. Clear up any misunderstandings

As a rule, people are terrible communicators. They forget to ask important questions, misinterpret your answers, filter your responses through their biases, make incorrect assumptions, and so on. As a result, interviewers can form inaccurate negative opinions about you purely because of shortcomings in their communication skills.

For example, I often have to inform a candidate that they didn't get a job because the manager concluded that they lacked a certain skill such as Java. The candidate responds in surprise, "But she never asked me any Java questions. I'm an expert in Java."

Don't ever let this happen to you! Don't miss out on a job because of a misunderstanding that could have been easily corrected if you had just had the courage to uncover it.

The surest way to find out about such misunderstandings is through an attempt to close. Smart salespeople use this technique all the time. Often the sale only starts in earnest after the prospective customer says, "No."

3. Move the ball over the goal line before anything bad can happen

The longer it takes for the company to decide to make you an offer, the more opportunities there can be for something to go wrong:

- A better candidate comes along.
- The company institutes a hiring freeze.
- They decide to reorganize and eliminate the position.

If you have a firm commitment to move forward and a timetable for doing so, this is much less likely to happen.

4. Uncover any hidden concerns

Interviewers can have concerns about you that they are reluctant to share for whatever reason. It makes no difference if these concerns are major or minor. Any one of them can cost you the job. Some are fatal to your chances and cannot be overcome. Others are relatively small and could be explained away but only if you uncover and handle them during the interview. Afterwards, it is too late. The surest way to uncover these hidden concerns is through a trial close. Again, often the sale only starts in earnest after the prospect first says, "No."

5. Salvage a failed interview

It is inevitable that you will blow an occasional interview question. Sometimes you know it, but many times you are unaware of having done so. When you attempt to close, you can uncover this problem and have a second chance to answer the question correctly. The second attempt may not be any more successful than the first, but it is always worth the effort. Later in this document, I will discuss how you do this.

Why People Fail to Close

The number one reason people fail to ask the closing questions is a fear of rejection. They do not want to hear the word "No" in person. They would rather get the rejection via email. Don't let this be you! Suppress your fear and you will be amazed at the positive results.

The second reason people fear asking closing questions is that they are worried about coming off as being pushy. *Telling* people that they need to make a quick decision to hire you – that would be pushy. However, that is not my advice here. What I am suggesting is that you ask questions. There is a world of difference between *asking* and *telling*. *Asking* the interviewer for their decision or feedback is *never* pushy. Instead, it is a display of self-confidence and interest in the job.

No interviewer will ever say to you, "I was ready to hire you until you asked for my feedback." The likeliest reason they would feel uncomfortable with the question is that they did not want to reject you to your face.

If you are still not convinced, think about the reverse situation where the interviewer asks *you* the vital closing question. For example, suppose that you are interviewing for a job in which you are very interested. The interviewer concludes the interview by saying to you, "Bill, we think you would be a great asset to our team. We like your skills and attitude and would really enjoy working with you. If we made you an offer, would you like to join our firm?" How could you possibly be offended by such a question?

Cultural Factors

In some cultures, direct questions are *never* asked. If your cultural background is like this, you will have a conditioned aversion to asking for immediate feedback, let alone a commitment, in the interview. I want to reassure you that there are no such cultural taboos in America. In fact, you may have noticed that Americans are so very direct in their communication that sometimes they can step over the line into rudeness. So, be reassured that closing, when done with skill and tact, is never rude and should not cause offense. In fact, because you demonstrated the confidence to ask for feedback, you will be thought of more positively. People will assume that your confidence in closing comes from your confidence in your abilities and will give you higher marks for job competence.

Closing Is Easy

Closing is the simplest and easiest skill to learn and implement. It only requires you to have the courage to ask a few questions. These questions can be one of two types – soft closes and direct closes.

Soft Closes

Soft closes are questions that primarily ask the interviewer for their opinion rather than for their commitment. Here are some examples:

- "Do you think I would be a good addition to your team?"
- "Are my skills and experience a good match for your needs?"
- "How well do I fit what you need in this position?"
- "Would you like me on your team?"
- "Do you think I would be a helpful addition to the project?"

Direct Closes

Direct closes ask the interviewer for a commitment. Examples of direct closes:

- "Can I expect an offer from you?"
- "Will you recommend me for this position?"
- "Would you like us to move to the next step in the hiring process?"
- "When should we meet again?"

When to Use Soft vs. Direct Closes

You should start first with soft closes to understand the lay of the land. If you get a positive response to your soft close, then move to a direct close and ask for a commitment. For example:

"Do you think I would be a good addition to your team?"

If the answer is yes: "I'm very glad to hear that because I think so, too, and I want to work here. When should we meet again?"

I recommend that you think of additional closing questions, both soft and direct, and rehearse them before you go on any interviews. In this way, you will be fully prepared to be a polished closer in your interviews.

Closing Starts When You Meet the Interviewer

To close effectively at the end of the interview, you need to lay a foundation at the beginning of the interview as follows:

1. Understand today's interview schedule and agenda

Once you have broken the ice at the start of the interview, find out from the interviewer how much time they have budgeted to meet with you and also what will happen in the interview. You will need this information later.

2. Ask the interviewer for their objectives for the interview

It is important that you understand what the interviewer wants to walk out with at the end of the interview.

"I just wanted to meet you," is not an objective. Find out why they wanted to meet you. Here are some sample questions:

"What would you like to accomplish in the next 45 minutes?"
"What would you like to walk away with at the end of our meeting?"

3. Understand the hiring process

Make sure you know what steps you have to successfully complete to get the job offer, including the ones following today's interview. Example questions:

"Can you please outline your hiring process for me?"
"If you are satisfied with the outcome of today's interview, what will be the next step in the process? What are the steps after that?"

Make sure that you get a statement of concrete actions, usually ones that pertain to you in some way, rather than some vague comments like, "I'll be reviewing my interview notes and will get back to you with a decision." Such statements contain no information that is useful to you. So, dig deeper:

"If you were to decide that I passed today's interview, where would we go from here?"

The answer to this, or similar questions, will let you know what to ask for at the end of the interview when you close.

4. State your objectives for the interview

As appropriate to the situation, inform the interviewer clearly and concretely what you would like to accomplish in the meeting. Here are a couple of examples:

- *Early-stage interview:* "I would like to learn more about the position to confirm that this is a role that I can successfully fill and in which I can make a positive contribution."

- *Late-stage interview:* "I am very excited about this role, your business and your company's future, and I very much want to be a part of that. My goal today is to gain your support and recommendation to bring me on board and be part of the team."

Does this sound bold and pushy to you? If so, think of the reverse situation in which you are meeting the company CEO who says to you at the beginning of the interview:

"Sarah, I have spoken to the people you have met so far, and everyone gives you high praise. My goal today is to answer any remaining questions you may have and to persuade you to come aboard."

How would you feel in Sarah's situation? You would feel pretty good, wouldn't you? In this same way, a hiring manager likes to hear positive comments from a candidate in whom they are interested.

However, be careful not to reveal objectives that may be off-putting to the interviewer. For example, if one of your objectives for the interview is to put some concerns to rest, do not express these to the interviewer. If you come across as nervous or hesitant, you will set off alarm bells and cause them to be hesitant about you.

Here is an illustration of how to handle a typical reservation you may have. If you are worried that some of the people on the team may be difficult to work with, don't say, "I want to make sure that I can work with Raj and Melissa because I have a concern about their work styles." A negative-sounding statement like this will almost certainly get you eliminated. Instead, ask to spend more one-on-one time with Raj and Melissa prior to accepting an offer. Put your request in positive terms:

"Since Raj, Melissa and I would be working very closely together, I would like some one-on-one time with each. I would like to learn their expectations of me as well as their work and communication styles so that I know what I need to do to fit in well with them."

How to Close at the End of the Interview

As the interview progresses, monitor the time in an unobtrusive manner. With about 10 minutes left in the allotted time, begin the closing process. The reason for starting this early is to allow time for you to uncover and remove any of the interviewer's concerns.

Step 1 – Assume a positive outcome.

Unless you have specifically been told that you are not a candidate, assume that you have successfully passed the interview and that you will be going on to the next step, whatever that may be.

Step 2 – Tell the interviewer that you want the job.

It is essential that you give the interviewer positive feedback. People are not mind readers. If they don't hear you explicitly say that you are interested in the position and why, they may decide that you are lukewarm on the opportunity. Don't assume that your smiles and head nodding are sufficient. So, tell the person explicitly that you want the job and give a few (2-4) *substantive* reasons. These reasons could include challenging work, learning opportunity, responsibility, or compatible colleagues. Don't include salary, benefits or superficial reasons like, "I love your free lunches."

When you tell people that you want the job, you increase your odds of being selected. This is because human psychology is such that people form more favorable opinions of those who show an interest in and a liking for them, as opposed to indifference towards them. So, I cannot stress enough how important it is to tell people that you want the job and to give your reasons.

If you are uncomfortable with my advice to say you want the job before you have fully made up your mind, all I can say is that it is really important that you get past your discomfort.

First, saying that you want to work at a company does not commit you to accept just any offer from them. If their offer is not satisfactory or if you uncover some other deal breaker later, you will not be obligated to take their offer just because earlier you said you wanted the job.

Second, saying that you want the position before you are 100% certain that you do is not dishonest. At this point, you are merely expressing your enthusiasm and interest. To be sure, if you are 100% convinced that you would hate to work there, then don't lie.

However, even if you are only 2% convinced that it is a good opportunity, come across as 100% positive. You can always change your mind later from a "yes" to a "no." The reverse is not true. If they assume you are not interested, they will cross you off their list. Even if you call back the next day to say that you thought it over and are interested, it will be too late because by then they will have moved on to the next candidate.

Step 3 – Close.

You have given them your feedback and stated your interest. Now it is their turn to do the reverse. First, start with a soft close that relates directly to their objectives stated at the beginning of the interview; e.g.,

"You stated at the beginning of the interview that one of your goals today was to assess my ability to succeed in this position. So, now I would like to ask your opinion. Are you satisfied that I could perform up to your expectations?"

Closing Scenarios

There are only three possible answers from the interviewer to your closing question: yes, no or maybe (or other non-committal answer). Here is how to handle each type of response:

1. "Yes" Answer

Great!! A "yes" is exactly what you want. Your response should be as follows:

- Express your enthusiasm for the positive response.
- If the interviewer had stated any other objectives for the interview, ask a soft closing question for each of those as well.
- If you get a negative or non-committal answer to any soft close, handle it as suggested below.
- If you get a positive answer to all your soft closes, go for a direct close and establish a firm action plan and timetable. Your close should include who should do what and when. For example, you will contact your references and provide the list to the employer within 48 hours. They will then contact the references right away. If the references are satisfactory, you will receive the oral offer immediately and the written offer within three days after that.
- Leave immediately. You have made the sale. Don't hang around to possibly make them change their minds.

2. "No" Answer

If you get a "No," don't stand up and slink out the door. All is not necessarily lost. The "No" means that the interviewer has a concern about you. Sometimes these concerns can be eliminated, *but only while you are still in the room.* Instead of giving up, find out what the concern is. That is what skilled salespeople do.

"Obviously, I'm disappointed. May I ask why not?"

As the interviewer discusses their concerns:

- Listen to them carefully and restate them in a question form to make sure you understand the concern.
- Decide if the concern is *easy to handle* or *difficult*.

Here is an example response to a stated concern:

"Just to make sure that I understand you correctly, are you saying that you are concerned that this is a position that may not hold sufficient challenge for me?"

Responding to Easily Handled Concerns

Easily handled concerns are usually the result of a miscommunication; e.g., the interviewer forgot to ask you a question, they misunderstood your answer, or formed an incorrect impression from some non-verbal cue. You should be able to eliminate these concerns 100% of the time.

To handle these easy concerns, again restate the concern in the form of a question to confirm that you understand it. Then answer it directly by correcting the interviewer's mistaken conclusion. For example, if the interviewer states a concern that you lack a certain skill that, in fact, you do possess, respond with evidence that proves that you do have that skill.

Responding to Difficult Concerns

Sometimes the interviewer's concern is legitimate; e.g., your salary is above their planned budget, or they may be looking for a skill that you don't have or do not have enough of. In this case, first restate the concern in a question form to make sure you understand it correctly. Then try to minimize the deficiency and point out compensating strengths that you have which are important to the position. Additionally, emphasize your confidence that you will be able to get up to speed in the position and be productive quickly. You may not always be successful at this, but you will be surprised at how often a persistent, confident approach will overcome the interviewer's concerns.

Remember that perfect candidates are rare and that, even if one were available with 100% of the desired skills and experience, they would not necessarily want the assignment, because there would be no challenge, personal growth or new learning in the position for them. You may even point this out to the interviewer, if appropriate, and emphasize that what you find attractive about the position is the opportunity to learn new skills and that this would make you a good long-term employee.

Try Closing Again

As you discuss each of the interviewer's concerns, don't move on to the next one until you have gotten an agreement from the interviewer that the specific concern under discussion should not stand in the way of your getting an offer. If you are unsuccessful in overcoming one or more of the interviewer's concerns, you are unlikely to get hired. However, at least you will know why you did not get the job, and the information may help you do better on the next interview.

If you are successful in overcoming the interviewer's concerns, then try a direct closing question again, possibly using a different phraseology. Again, closing means asking for a commitment that you be taken to the next step; e.g., to be called back for another interview, or to be made an offer.

3. Handling the Non-Committal Interviewer ("Maybe" Answer)

Many interviewers will be reluctant to give you feedback. Common responses are, "I'd like to think about it and get back to you," "I'd like to discuss it with the other people you met," or "I have several more people to interview." Don't settle for these kinds of responses. Be gracious but be persistent. One way to do this is to say, "I don't want to put you on the spot by asking you for a commitment, but I *would* like to know how you think I did. At this point, I am simply asking for your opinion."

Be aware though, this kind of questioning *will* put some pressure on the interviewer. However, that's OK. You have just invested several hours of your time preparing for the interview, driving to the interview location, and enduring their questions. The *least* that you deserve is honest feedback. So, continue with your questions by first asking for positive feedback.

"What do you think are the positives that I bring to the position?" Wait for an answer. If none is forthcoming, there is virtually no chance that you will get the job. At this point, there is not much more that you can do.

If the interviewer does have positive things to say about you, reinforce these impressions. Do this as follows:

- Agree with the positive comments; e.g., "You're right. I've always been known as a very effective project manager."
- If possible, state an additional example from past accomplishments that reinforces this point.

This technique of agreeing with the interviewer and expanding on their comment is called a "Support Statement." It is described more fully in Chapter 10.

If the interviewer has several positive things to say about you, the following is not necessary. But if they struggle to come up with more than one or two items, you should try to help them along by reminding them of positive comments they may have made earlier in the interview or areas where you think you did well. For example:

"I got the impression that you liked the fact that I received two promotions in under three years at my current employer. What did you like about this?"

If they reply with a favorable comment, reinforce it as above. The sample advanced close in Chapter 11 has further examples of this technique.

If you do get some positive comments from the interviewer and have discussed all of them, then it is essential that you also probe for potential problems; e.g., "Do you have any concerns?," "Do you have any reservations about me for the position?" or "Is there anything that would stand in the way of your recommending me (or inviting me for the next round of interviews or making me an offer)?" If the interviewer states some concerns, handle them as above.

Hidden Concerns

Be aware that a non-committal answer is sometimes used by interviewers as a smokescreen to hide something they may be embarrassed about or simply uncomfortable telling a candidate directly. Common examples are:

- Lack of interpersonal chemistry – There are times when two people just don't click! Interviewers will rarely admit this to a candidate, and there is nothing that can be done about this.
- Discrimination – The interviewer can be biased against a candidate for any number of reasons. Age, gender, ethnicity, and race are among the most common. Interviewers will never admit their prejudice, and there is nothing an interviewee can do to overcome bigotry.

If the interviewer has any of these or similar hidden concerns, no amount of probing or closing effort will succeed in overcoming them or even uncovering them. Nevertheless, you should continue to close because such hidden concerns only occur in a minority of situations. So, your efforts to be a good closer *will* pay off most of the time.

Summary

Closing, as I said earlier, is easy. All you need to do is ask the closing questions. The difficult part comes in handling the interviewer's concerns. How well you uncover and handle their concerns will depend on:

- Your confidence level,
- Your interviewing skills,
- The nature of the concern; i.e., is it a misunderstanding or something substantive.

To gain confidence and skill, practice the advice in this section before you go for any live interviews. You can do this with a trusted colleague who has experience interviewing prospective employees, your spouse or a friend. You can even do this in front of a bathroom mirror. Tennis players hit thousands of serves on the practice court before they play in a tournament. In the same way, off-line practice will make you a better interviewer in every way.

A Final Note About Closing

I have coached thousands of people in closing over the years. Not even one has come back to me to say, "That was the worst advice I've heard from anyone. I tried to close, and it cost me the job." On the other hand, I have numerous instances of positive feedback such as this true story. "I was worried about asking for feedback. So, the first time I tried to close, I said to the interviewer, 'The recruiter told me to ask you this.' When I got a good reaction from the first interviewer, I was much more confident in the next interviews, and your advice worked beautifully. In fact, I received two offers out of the next three interviews." So, my guidance for you is that even if you have misgivings, ask the closing questions. You can only gain from the attempt, and you may be amazed at the positive results.

2. Knowing Your Product

What Makes You a Valuable Employee

As I said earlier, top salespeople know their products thoroughly – and so should you. In this case, the product is you. So, it is essential that you understand what attributes you possess that would make you attractive to a potential employer.

Interviewers commonly ask the question, "Why should I hire you?" You need to have a thorough and convincing answer to such a question, and you should anticipate that the answer may vary from interview to interview. So, it is important that you understand both what would make you a good employee overall and also for specific opportunities. Therefore, before you do anything else, make a list of 40-60 of your work-related features. Divide these into three groups:

- Personal Qualities
- Transferable Skills
- Domain-Specific Knowledge and Skills

40-60 may seem like an excessive number, but it isn't. To prove my point, look at this ready-made list of examples you can use to start your own list.

Personal Qualities

Hardworking
Self-starter
Fast learner
Trustworthy
Team player
Reliable
Intelligent
Creative thinker
Collaborative worker
Disciplined
Determined
Honest
Possess a positive attitude
Direct in your communication style (apolitical)
Deal well with stress
Adaptable and flexible
Realistic in your expectations
Emotionally stable
Accepting of others' values, cultures and opposing views
Deal well with conflicts and able to resolve them in a positive manner

Transferable Skills

       Preparing and delivering presentations
       Effectively dealing with customers
       Delivering training
       Team leadership
       Project management
       Excellent written skills
       Clear oral communication skills
       Good organizer of work for others
       Personally well-organized
       Expert negotiator
       Good problem solver
       Inspiring leader of others
       Skilled people manager
       Skilled at selecting office space and negotiating leases

Domain Specific Knowledge

This list will depend on the field or fields in which you have worked; e.g., investment banking, discrete manufacturing, retail, automotive, wholesale distribution, real estate, healthcare, etc. Analyze your skills and knowledge specific to each domain in which you have worked and list them here; e.g., those only applicable to investment banking.

Backing Up Your Claims

After making the list, think of at least one (preferably two or three) concrete examples of your past accomplishments that illustrate each of the above qualities. It is not necessary to think of a separate example for each item. One particular project or position may have drawn on most of your strengths and can illustrate them well. However, make sure you have at least five different substantive accomplishments for all the above points combined.

If You Work in High Tech

My practice is based in the Silicon Valley/San Francisco Bay Area, and I specialize in high-tech jobs. So, I give slightly different advice to technology workers. If you work in high tech, you should organize your list into the following categories:

- Personal Qualities
- Technical Skills
- Job-Related Knowledge and Skills

Here are examples of things that you should include in your list:

Personal Qualities

    Identical to the list above.

Technical Skills

    Platforms (Java, iOS, Android, Linux, Windows, Amazon Web Services, etc.)
    Programming Languages (Java, Objective-C, C++, Python, RoR, C#, etc.)
    Databases (Oracle, MySQL, PostgreSQL, SQL Server, etc.)
    Big Data Technologies (NoSQL, Hadoop, MapReduce, Cassandra, etc.)
    Mobile Technologies (iOS, Android, Objective-C, Java, Sencha, Swift, etc.)
    Development Tools
    Middleware
    ERP, CRM or other application packages
    Design and Development Methodologies (Agile, Scrum, Pair Programming)

Job-Related Knowledge and Skills

    Design
    Programming
    Debugging
    Writing documentation
    Testing and integration
    Machine Learning Algorithms
    Continuous Integration
    Test Automation
    UI/UX Design
    Functional Business Areas Expert; e.g., Supply Chain Management, CRM
    Preparing and delivering presentations
    Customer interface
    Delivering training
    Team leadership
    Project management
    Excellent written skills
    Clear oral communication skills
    Good organizer of work for others
    Personally well-organized
    Expert negotiator
    Good problem solver
    Inspiring leader of others
    Skilled people manager

Using Your List in Interviews

Obviously, you won't be trotting out all of your 40-60 assets in every interview. You will only be presenting those that are the most relevant to the opportunity and of greatest interest to the interviewer. In the Controlling the Interview section, I will discuss how to do this.

3. Controlling the Interview

What Does It Mean to Control the Interview?

Control in an interview means that you assume responsibility for the agenda and flow of the conversation. The reason you should assume control is to ensure that you lead the interviewer to the decisions and actions that you want; e.g., making you a job offer or inviting you back for another interview. You do this by doing more listening than talking during the interview.

The idea that you mostly listen in an interview is counter-intuitive to most people. Almost everyone thinks that the way to succeed in interviews is to be good at answering questions. Also, the perception of what makes a good salesperson is that they are great talkers. While answering questions well and being articulate are obviously important in both interviews and sales, what distinguishes great salespeople is their ability to listen. In fact, 80% of sales success comes from great listening skills whether you are selling software or yourself. As in a sales call, the best way to be doing most of the listening in an interview is to be asking most of the questions.

Please note, when I suggest that you control the interview, I am not advising you to be overbearing or bossy. That is not how successful sales professionals work. Instead, I am suggesting that you gently but firmly take charge of the flow of the conversation. Interview control is not an easy skill to master and requires you to be better prepared and more skilled at asking questions than the interviewer. Becoming proficient at using questions for control can only come from focused study, thought, and practice on your part. In this section, I will show you how to get started with gaining this expertise.

Some people may be hesitant about taking my advice about controlling the interview. They may be apprehensive at the thought of taking responsibility in the interview, or they may not feel confident in their interviewing skills. If you are one of them, I'd like to give you a few words of reassurance. First, there are different degrees of control by the interviewee from some control to 100% control. You don't have to reach the 100% mark to benefit from attempting to exert some control of the conversation. Second, even if you only implement the pre-interview preparation part of the advice in this section, you will perform better in the interview. Everyone, including the timid interviewee, has the ability to prepare well for interviews. So, read on.

Why it is Important for You to Control the Interview

If you are going to have consistent success in your interviews, you will need to focus on controlling them because:

1. It is your job to sell yourself, not the company's job to select you.

It is a fundamental principle of effective sales of complex products (and people are about as complex as a product can get) that it is the *job of the salesperson to make the sale* and not the responsibility of the customer to select and buy the product. I would like you to stop and think about this for a minute, for it is the guiding principle of this entire document. This principle requires you to turn on its head the way you think about the roles of interviewer and interviewee. Most people think that their task in interviews is to answer questions, as in an oral exam, and then *be selected*. Simply answering questions is *not* the way to sell yourself. To illustrate what I mean, consider the following example:

Let's pretend that you are shopping for a new flat-screen TV. It is a subject that you don't know much about other than the names of the major manufacturers. You show up at a large electronics retail store, with dozens of TVs on display, looking to find the one that is right for you. The first salesperson you approach for help says to you, "Take a look at what's on display. Look at the descriptions and features for each. Research them on your smartphone, if you need to. Ask me as many questions as you like, and then let me know which one you want."

You leave this person and approach a second salesperson. This one takes a completely different approach. She begins by asking you a detailed list of questions such as where you would like to use the TV and what you would like to use it for besides basic TV viewing. After an extensive consultative interview, she shows you two or three of the dozens on display and explains to you the relative ability of each to meet what you're looking for. She asks your opinion about which appeals to you most. She may even recommend one above the others. Then she takes your credit card.

In your opinion, which of these two approaches would lead to greater sales success? The second, wouldn't you agree?

In the same way, you don't want to leave it up to the interviewer to try to figure out whether or not you are a fit for the position. It is *your* job to determine this. Once you determine that you are a good match, then your task is to convince the interviewer that your conclusion is correct. That, in a nutshell, is how you sell yourself in an interview.

2. Most interviewers wing it.

Most interviewers invest very little in preparing for an upcoming interview. In fact, it is a rare interviewer who puts together more than a handful of questions in advance of the interview. Often, they barely even skim the person's resume. It is very common for an interviewer to sit down with a candidate and say, "Here is your resume. Here is the job description. Let's talk." From there the dialog takes off in some random directions. Random discussions lead to random results. If you want an organized, structured, businesslike discussion and a predictable outcome in your favor, you will have to take responsibility for controlling the agenda and the discussion. An ill-prepared interviewer will usually be happy to let you control the conversation, so be prepared and take charge.

3. Many, if not most, interviewers get no training.

Virtually no one you will be interviewing with has attended a course, or even read a book, on how to interview people. They are unlikely even to have ever had any informal instruction from a manager or colleague. Most interviewers learn their interviewing skills through trial and error. If the person has never done any hiring, the level of instruction they are likely to have gotten from their boss is, "Here's the resume. Talk to her. Find out what she knows about mortgage-backed securities." Inexperienced interviewers will make rookie mistakes, mistakes that can cost you the job. Protect yourself against their amateurishness by taking control. You will, in fact, be doing the person a favor by relieving them of the pressure of being responsible for the interview.

4. You are at the interview to meet your goals, not just the interviewer's.

You need to think selfishly about each interview. You are there to have your needs met not just to answer a bunch of interview questions. Remember, your investment in the interview is usually far greater than the interviewer's. If you have taken the interview seriously, you may have spent many hours preparing. In contrast, it is a rare interviewer who spends more than a few minutes getting ready for an interview. At a minimum, you may have taken a vacation day and been the one to drive to the company's offices for the interview, rather than the other way around. You should expect a return on this investment by making sure that you get at least an equal opportunity to ask your questions and to achieve your objectives, not just the interviewer's. It is not rude to insist on this, and it should not hurt your chances to get the job.

Frankly, if I met an interviewer who just wanted to grill me without giving me at least equal time to get answers to my questions, I would almost certainly cross them off my list of potential employers. There are just too many negative explanations for such behavior and no positive ones. So, don't let yourself be quizzed extensively and then be shown the door with a "We'll let you know" on the way out. Stand up for yourself and make sure you meet your goals for the interview.

Control Starts With Preparation

Your control of an upcoming interview starts when you start preparing for the interview. Here are the steps to follow as you prepare:

1. Define your objectives for the interview.

Identify what you wish to get out of the upcoming interview. "Advance to the next stage in the hiring process" should always be your number one objective. Here are some other possible ones:

- Understand the hiring process.
- Get an offer.
- Determine if you can do the job.
- Pass a skills test.
- Build rapport with your future manager and colleagues.
- Understand the manager's expectations of you.
- Discover why you would want the job if offered it.
- Get a clear picture of what it would be like to work there.
- Resolve your concerns.
- Overcome the employer's concerns.
- Negotiate offer terms (late-stage interview).

A word of caution. The interview is *not* the time and place for you to make a decision about taking the job or even if you want to work there. "Decide on the offer" should *not* be on your list of objectives. The interview is where you *sell yourself and close*. The decision phase comes later when you are no longer on the hot seat and have time to analyze the information you have gathered and can carefully think through your decision.

2. Plan your strategy for the interview.

Analyze what you know about the position, the company and the environment in which you will be working. Think about which of your features would be most relevant to the position and why. Then plan how you can best present these features to convince the interviewer that you can do the job.

3. Prepare your pre-interview list of questions.

Once you have defined your objectives and thought about which of your features you should emphasize, start planning your interview questions. Each question should focus on either achieving an objective or leading the discussion in such a way that you will have a chance to present your features that are most relevant to the position. Think of your list of questions as if it were a flowchart where step one is to shake hands with the interviewer and the last step is your walking out of the interview with a commitment to move to the next step. On a high level, the flowchart should proceed as follows:

1. Find out what the company needs to be accomplished.
2. Identify how your skills and experience can help them get it done; i.e., how you can benefit the company.
3. Find out how working there would *benefit you.*

Later, I will discuss more specifically what questions to prepare and how to use them.

4. Anticipate objections.

Think about what concerns the interviewer might have regarding you as a candidate for the position. Some of these concerns might be ones applicable to any interview; e.g., gaps in your resume, short job stays, incomplete education. Other concerns could be specific to the position at hand; e.g., the job description requires ten years of a certain skill, and you only have five years.

It is not within the scope of this document to give you specific advice on how to handle each objection beyond what is contained in the section on "Closing." The most important thing I can add here is that if you know the objection will come up, don't wing it. Before the interview, prepare and rehearse responses that take each potential concern seriously but don't make you sound defensive. To help sharpen your replies, consult people who have had extensive interviewing experience for their advice and feedback on your answers.

Your List of Questions

Types of Questions

There are two main types of questions you will prepare prior to an interview: Discovery Questions and Leading Questions. There are other types of questions you may use, but I will explain those elsewhere.

Discovery questions are open-ended questions that cannot be answered in a single word or phrase. They invite the interviewer to talk at length and are most useful for gathering information. Another advantage of using open-ended questions is that while the interviewer is talking you cannot say anything that can cost you the job. Also, you will be under less stress while you are listening than when you are speaking, so you can bring your nervousness under control. A good technique is to start the discovery question with the phrase "Tell me about…." For example, "Tell me about the most important challenges you are facing in your supply chain."

Leading questions are sometimes also referred to as closed-ended questions. These are questions that can be answered in one word or with a short phrase. You should avoid leading questions in your pre-interview list of questions unless they serve a very important purpose and are absolutely essential. The problem with using too many leading questions is that you may come off as an attorney grilling a hostile witness. This style of questioning can harm rapport with the interviewer. Also, you will quickly run out of questions and will either lose control of the interview or be shown the door. Therefore, it is usually best to rephrase any leading questions as open-ended discovery questions; e.g., instead of asking, "How many employees are there in your organization?" ask "Tell me about how your group is organized."

There is, however, one excellent use for leading questions. If you discover during the interview that you have a skill or knowledge that would be particularly useful for the position for which you are interviewing, use leading questions to direct the conversation to your area of strength. For example:

You: "Are you satisfied with your level of finished goods inventory?"
Interviewer: "No, it is too high."
You: "Sounds like you would like to lower the level then, am I right?"
Interviewer: "Yes."
You: "At my current employer, I helped reduce finished goods inventory levels by 20%. Would you like to hear about that?"

By using a leading question, you have directed the conversation to talk about your strengths and have given yourself an opportunity to put your best foot forward.

Questions to Avoid

Do not ask questions about salary, other compensation, or benefits. Discussing these topics during an interview will not help you get the job but can certainly get you eliminated from consideration. Salary and other compensation should be discussed only after they have made the decision to hire you, at which point you will enter the negotiation phase of the hiring process. Benefits should be discussed only if the interviewer brings them up or after they have made you an offer.

Avoid negative-sounding questions such as, "What are the problems with this project?" You can discuss such things but phrase them in a positive way; e.g., "What are the challenges that need to be overcome in this project?" The word "challenge" lacks the negative connotation of the word "problem."

Never ask the question, "What are you looking for in a person for this position?" You're likely to get a long wish list of qualifications that don't match yours, yet you could still be qualified to do the job. Better alternatives:

- "What skills and qualities would best enable a person to succeed in the job?"
- "Who is your best person in a similar job? What do you think makes them good at their job?"

As they respond to your question by describing the qualities that these real people possess, take the opportunity to show how you are like the person being described.

Using your Questions During the Interview

As you prepare your list of questions, make sure you have at least 20 discovery questions prior to the interview. They should consist of a minimum of 5 each about the company, the department or project, the interviewer, and the position. The benefits of having questions prepared are:

- By being the one asking the questions you will maintain control of the interview.
- The answers provide you with valuable information for knowing how to best present your skills and also for evaluating any potential offer.
- They are an excellent way of showing enthusiasm and interest in the company and the position.
- They create a favorable impression of you by showing that you are prepared, organized and serious about the interview.

In case it is not already clear to you, make certain that you write these questions out and that you take the list with you. Chapter 5 contains a list of example interview questions that will help you get started. By writing out your questions, you ensure that you:

- Formulate better questions.
- Organize them in a more logical and effective sequence.
- Won't forget the questions, because you will take the list with you and use them during the interview.

An effective way to use these questions in the interview is to memorize the first one or two questions to get the interviewer talking. After the interview is underway, ask the person, "Do you mind if I take some notes?" No one will object. After all, interviewers also take notes, usually on your resume. Then, take out your notepad, have your questions on one side and take your notes on the other.

Interview Structure

Rather than having interviews that are spontaneous conversations that follow no consistent path or pattern or are dictated by the interviewer, you should have a standard structured interview. Your interview should consist of the following five sections in this order:

1. Establish Rapport
2. Define the Schedule, Agenda and Objectives for the Interview
3. Explore and Confirm a Mutual Fit
4. Close
5. Leave

The specifics of the first four sections will vary from interview to interview. However, they should occur in the order defined above, and you should not skip any steps.

1. Establish Rapport

Before you go for control in the interview by launching into your questions or jumping into answering the interviewer's questions, build some rapport with the interviewer. How exactly to do this and how much time this will take will vary widely. You should not skip this step with anyone you meet from executives to the receptionist.

The easiest ways to connect with others is with shared experiences, interests or people in common. So, always make an effort to research every person you expect to interview with on LinkedIn and via Google. Look for things that you might have in common and lead with these at the beginning of the interview. If you don't have anything in common, you can try some of the following:

- If I'm speaking with the founder of a startup, I usually start with, "What gave you the idea for the company and how did you get it started?"
- If I notice that they seem to have a lot of pictures of a hobby such as sailing, fishing, horseback riding, etc., I will ask them about their hobby.
- If I find on Google that they are active in some civic activities, I will think of a question to get them talking about that.

This rapport-building stage is important for several reasons. First, it changes the dynamic of the conversation from an impersonal applicant-interviewer relationship, with the interviewer being dominant, to two people getting to know each other on a peer level. Secondly, interviewers don't recommend hiring anyone they don't like, and candidates don't accept offers from managers they dislike. So, besides establishing the nuts and bolts of qualifications, you and the interviewer will need to confirm a personality fit. The rapport-building stage initiates this process.

2. Define the Schedule, Agenda and Objectives for the Interview

I have already covered this in detail in the Closing section of this document. Here is a reminder:

- Understand today's interview schedule and agenda
- Ask the interviewer for their objectives for the interview
- Understand the hiring process
- State your objectives for the interview, but only as appropriate

3. Explore and Confirm a Mutual Fit

This section will consume the greatest portion of the time allotted for the interview. Each interview will be different in how this section will flow, so there is not enough space here to cover all the possibilities. But your overall strategy in the interview should be to:

1. Discover the hiring manager's need.
2. Determine for yourself how you can satisfy it.

3. Convince the interviewer that you are right in your conclusion that you can do the job.

Remember, it is the salesperson's job to decide what the customer needs and not the other way around. In this case, you are the salesperson, so you have to assume the burden of discovering and confirming that there is a mutual fit between you and the company. The way you discover this is through the skilled use of questioning techniques. This is where your list of pre-interview questions will come into play.

Let me stress again how important it is that you determine for yourself that you are a good candidate for the position and why this is true. If you are not confident that you are a match for the job, how can you persuade the interviewer? Obviously, you can't.

4. Close

To repeat what I said in the Closing section, unless you are 100% convinced that you don't want the job, always, always attempt to close. Top-notch salespeople and top-notch interviewers always close.

To take this a step further, until you feel completely confident in your closing abilities, I recommend that you close at every interview because you will need the practice. This includes the interviews where you don't want the job. Just leave out the part about wanting to work at the company. The reason I am advising that you close even if you don't want the job is that if you make an error in closing, you won't be losing anything through your mistake.

5. Leave

If you are successful in your close, don't hang around for needless chit-chat. Unnecessary small talk at the end only opens the door to the possibility that you will say something that the interviewer can misinterpret. The time for such conversation is after you have returned the signed acceptance letter.

Maintaining Control in the Interview

Many interviewers will be happy to let you control the interview, especially if they have not done much preparation themselves. However, you can frequently run into an interviewer who starts firing questions at you as soon as you sit down in the meeting. Being subjected to a grilling can easily throw you off your game plan and could take you down the road to failure. So, you will most likely want to get back to your agenda as quickly and as deftly as possible.

I have learned a technique for this that works nearly 100% of the time. It is contained in the book "How to Master the Art of Selling" by Tom Hopkins. He calls it the "Porcupine Technique." Here's what he says about it:

Imagine a little porcupine snuffling around in the brush with all its sharp long needles sticking out. If somebody put one in a sack and threw it at you, what would you do?

You'd throw it right back.

The porcupine is the technique of answering a prospect's question with a question of your own that maintains your control of the interview and allows you to lead into the next step of your selling sequence.

You may ask, "Won't prospects be annoyed unless I give them specific answers to their questions?"

Here's my porcupine answer: "Why are you so fearful of annoying prospects when your main concern should be to close them so that they can enjoy the benefits of your offering?"

Here is an example of how you might use the porcupine technique in an interview.

Let's suppose that as soon as you sit down to meet, the interviewer fires out the first question. "Tell me about yourself." Instead of responding directly, try a porcupine question. "Well, there's a lot to tell. What was there in my resume that particularly interested you and we can start with that?" Notice how I have taken the initiative away from the interviewer and I am now back in control.

To cite another example, during the middle of the interview, the interviewer asks, "What do you know about negotiating outsourcing manufacturing contracts?" This is a broad subject, and you don't want to go into a thirty-minute lecture on it. Instead of responding immediately, try a porcupine question: "I've got quite a bit of experience with this. Can you please tell me the specific need you have in this area, and I'll focus my answer on that?" Again, notice how I am back in control. Remember, it is up to you, the one doing the selling, to control the interview, and the person asking the questions is the one in control. So, as much as possible, you should aim to be asking questions to get the interviewer talking.

To be sure, you cannot go through an entire interview without answering questions. So, I am not advising you to deflect every question and withhold information. However, you don't necessarily have to answer every question thrown at you nor do you have to answer them all immediately when asked. When and whether or not you answer a question will depend on what would be the best response to achieve your interview goals. If an immediate answer will keep your strategy on track or you can provide a good answer, by all means answer immediately. However, if answering immediately may hurt you or take you off track, then use the porcupine technique to re-assert your control of the interview.

General Strategy for Answering Interview Questions

You will encounter many types of questions from interviewers, from the practical to the ridiculous. The variety is much too great to cover them here. Plus, there are plenty of other sources for advice on this subject. So, I just want to cover some general points here.

Broad Questions

If you encounter a question that's very broad in nature and could be answered at great length, don't immediately answer it. Instead, ask clarifying questions to narrow down the scope of the question and to find out why the question is relevant to the position at hand. Porcupine questions are a good way to accomplish this.

Another important reason for asking clarifying questions is because you want to make sure that your answer is responsive to the question the interviewer had in mind. I have seen many instances when the interviewer asks one question, the candidate misunderstands the question and answers a completely different question. When this response is off-target the interviewer, instead of correcting the misunderstanding, simply rejects the candidate. To avoid this problem, first ask the clarifying questions. Then, after you have answered the question, ask specifically "Did I answer the question that you asked?"

Yes/No or Narrowly Defined Questions

Interviewers have hot buttons on narrow topics and will ask you questions that require either a yes/no or one-word answer; e.g., "Are you willing to travel?," "Are you willing to work overtime?," or "Do you have experience with macros in Excel?" Your first strategy for responding should be to give a positive response, if possible. For example, in the case of the travel question, you should answer "Yes, I can travel on business. Can you please describe to me the extent and nature of the travel?" Did you notice the porcupine question at the end?

If the question relates to a skill that you don't have, first ask a clarifying question. "Is that skill important to the position?" and then listen to the response. Many times, the employer will say, "No. It is not required. I was just interested in whether or not you had it." In other words, don't assume that just because you don't have a particular skill or knowledge you won't get the job. On the other hand, if the skill is a requirement and you are not particularly proficient in it, then try to ask clarifying questions to understand to what extent your lack might hold you back from getting the position. Then handle the interviewer's concern in the way that I described under 'Responding to Difficult Concerns' in the Closing section of this document.

To emphasize this point, if you do have to answer "no" to a question, particularly when it relates to skills, try to put a positive spin on your answer by directing attention to related skills that you do have and/or pointing out your compensating strengths that are relevant to the position. Also make a note that this might cause the interviewer concern and be prepared to address this item at the end of the interview during your close.

Listening to the Interviewer

As the interviewer is talking, you will use two forms of listening: Passive Listening and Active Listening.

When you listen to an opera singer perform, you show your respect and interest by staying quiet and listening attentively. This is Passive Listening.

While Passive Listening is a part of sales, there is a more effective technique for building rapport called Active Listening.

In Active Listening, instead of just nodding and smiling while the interviewer speaks, you listen attentively to both verbal and body language and then repeat back the main content of what the interviewer said. The two chief benefits of Active Listening are that it helps build rapport and can clear up any misunderstandings. Chapter 10 goes into more detail on this subject.

There are two particularly good situations for using Active Listening. The first is when you hear something that you like. In this case, repeat what the interviewer said with enthusiasm and let the person know that this is something you like and are very interested in. The second case is when the interviewer talks about a problem or need that they have that you can solve. In this case use Active Listening to repeat the problem and then state that you can help them with it. Again, Chapter 10 has some examples of this.

My overall advice is that you use Active Listening at every opportunity. Just don't interrupt or talk over the interviewer.

4. Putting It All Together

Knowing How to Interview Is an Essential Life Skill

Virtually nobody likes job hunting. However, it is an unavoidable necessity of life because job security is a thing of the past.

Just a few decades ago, it was possible for a person to graduate from college, receive a job offer from a large corporation such as HP, IBM or GE, spend their entire working life at that company, and then retire with a generous pension. However, that life model went out with the rotary phone.

By contrast, a person entering the workforce today will most likely have to look for a new job several times throughout their working life. Therefore, today nearly everyone needs two sets of skills to succeed professionally. The first set consists of the skills that each person will use every day to maintain their employment and earn their income. The second set is the one they will need for finding a job because it is a virtual certainty they will be looking for a new position every few years whether they want to or not. It is also a fact that, unless a person is in sales, the skills they will need to succeed at job searching will be very different from the skills that they will be using to excel in their career. A job search takes them out of their comfort zone and requires them to perform tasks at which they have very little experience, such as selling themselves in an interview. This discomfort is one of the reasons why people dislike job hunting.

Job hunting involves several activities. These include writing a resume, uncovering and pursuing job leads, arranging interviews, going on interviews, negotiating offers, evaluating jobs and offers, etc. The good news for you if you are looking for a job is that you can get help with most of these activities. For example, you can hire someone to write your resume, and you can enlist the help of recruiters to uncover job leads, arrange interviews and negotiate offers on your behalf. But the one thing that you cannot delegate to someone else is to go on the interview. Interviewing may put a lot of pressure on you for several reasons including the fact that by far the most important determinant of whether or not you get an offer is how well you do in the interview. That is why I wrote this guide – to help you become a skilled and confident interviewee. Moreover, I have focused on mostly giving advice that you are not likely to have seen elsewhere, advice that is highly effective, and advice that will give you a leg up on your competition.

This document is relatively short, but it is dense with information. So much so, that you may feel a bit overwhelmed and conclude that there is just too much for you to learn and put to use. I would like you to put that thought aside because you don't have to absorb everything in this document in one big gulp. You can study and implement my advice in small bite-sized chunks. In the next section, I will show you how to do that.

As you tackle the task of improving your interviewing skills, you may find your motivation flagging from time to time. When it does, I would like you to think about the fact that being skilled at interviews has important lifetime implications. By selling yourself more effectively, you can motivate interviewers to offer you more money, hire you for a position for which you are not fully qualified and select you above other attractive candidates. Your increased interviewing success can have huge positive effects on your lifetime earnings, career advancement and job satisfaction. Aren't these things that you want? If so, don't you think it's worth it to you to put in some effort and to move outside of your comfort zone?

Your Step-By-Step Implementation Plan

Now that you have decided that you want to be better at interviewing, you can follow the following steps towards success. Complete them in the order presented below. You don't have to complete every step, and there is no deadline for doing so. However, it is essential that you complete at least the first five. I also strongly recommend that you work on the others as well, but they are not as critical.

Essential Steps

Step 1 – Close at every interview.

I can't say this too many times. Closing is by far the most important and most powerful thing that you can do differently in your interviews. I have coached thousands of people in closing, and everyone who has taken my recommendation to heart has come back with a success story. For example, my daughter started her first job out of college eighteen years ago. Since then she has attended around twenty interviews, received ten job offers, and is now working for her sixth employer. (On two occasions she received multiple job offers.) She has some natural advantages in interviews by being articulate, smart and competent. But most of all, she has taken my advice to heart and is a consistent, tenacious and effective closer. (If your father is a butcher, you get to eat a lot of steaks. If your father is a recruiter, you get a lot of interview coaching.) Furthermore, she has forwarded my interview tips documents to her friends who have also had success from incorporating closing into their interviews.

I am not suggesting that you will also achieve a 50% success rate on your interviews. However, even if your offer ratio today is only 20% or even 10%, you will noticeably improve your ratio by closing. Best of all, among all the advice contained in this document, closing is by far the easiest to implement. As I mentioned in that section, all you need to do is ask a few questions. So, just do it.

Step 2 – Know what makes you a valuable employee.

Implement fully my advice in Chapter 2. Don't just think about it but also write out what would make you a good employee along with proofs to back up your claims. Before each interview, study this list so that you know it by heart and think about which of your assets would be of interest to the particular interviewer.

Step 3 – Prepare your written objectives and questions prior to every interview.

You may not have the skill and confidence to take charge in an interview once you are on the hot seat. But there is absolutely no excuse for winging it. Everyone can, and should, write out their objectives and list of questions prior to every interview. The actual interview may not unfold exactly as you had planned, and you may only get to ask a small fraction of your questions. But the mental preparation will enable you to perform much better than you would have otherwise.

BTW I practice what I preach. I always prepare my list of objectives and questions prior to meeting with any client and have been doing so for decades. (See examples in Chapter 6.)

Step 4 – Try Active Listening.

Active Listening is something you should add to every interview starting with your next one. Practice a few times with a friend and then just go for it. You should notice an immediate improvement in your rapport with each person you meet.

Step 5 – Learn to handle the salary question.

Giving a wrong answer to the salary question is the easiest way to be eliminated early in the interview cycle or, at a minimum, to get less money that you could have. So, study my advice in Chapter 8 and work on improving your responses.

Optional Steps

Step 6 – Analyze your performance after each interview.

Professional athletes can review films of their performances with a coach to learn from their successes as well as failures and thus improve their skills. No such films of your interviews are possible, but you should still invest in the effort to learn from your past interviews. By reflecting on and analyzing each interview, you can reinforce those things that work, eliminate those that don't and also learn from any mistakes. Chapter 14 includes a suggested format for this analysis.

If you discover through your analyses that there are certain things that you do well, make note of them and try to incorporate them into as many of your interviews as possible.

Step 7 – Implement a structured interview.

Sticking to a structured interview is easier than you think. All you need to do is to be the one to ask the first question in the interview. The most natural way to do this is during the rapport-building process. Don't wait until you sit down. Instead, you can throw out one of your ice-breaking questions as you're walking from the lobby to the conference room or while you're standing up and shaking the interviewer's hand. If you take the initiative to do this, you will immediately be in control. From there, it will be an easy step for you to ask the interviewer their objectives for the interview and then follow this up by stating yours, if appropriate to do so. The flow of the rest of the interview will vary and will depend partially on your confidence level and how insistent the interviewer is on taking control. Regardless of the flow of the conversation, you should always complete the last two steps: close and then leave immediately.

Step 8 – Attempt to control each interview.

Being able to control every interview is a difficult skill to master, and you don't need to be perfect at this to be very successful in your interviews (as long as you close). However, many interviewers will make it easy for you to lead by failing to prepare. These interviewers will be more than happy to cede control to you if they see that you are prepared and have well-thought-out relevant questions. At minimum, test the waters with every interviewer by asking a question at the earliest opportunity and also at every appropriate moment during the interview.

You should also continue polishing your Active Listening skills at every interview until this becomes an unconscious part of your technique.

Step 9 – Improve your questioning and control skills.

As you gain experience in interviewing, your confidence should build. At this point, try to incorporate the porcupine technique into your repertoire. But try this in a mock interview with a friend before you try it in a live situation.

This phase of your learning will require many hours of practice in both real and simulated interviews. So, don't expect rapid improvement but do strive for continuous progress until you eventually reach the limit of your natural sales ability, which is something that everyone has. However, this probably won't occur before you have completed a minimum of one hundred interviews.

Step 10 – Try using the optional skills.

If you are confident in your abilities and want to push yourself to the maximum, then you can try the advanced topics discussed in Part 2 of this book. Fewer than 10% of the people reading this will be able to implement everything I suggest in this guide and, even then, only after much dedicated and focused practice. So, have realistic expectations of yourself and also give yourself credit for your efforts and technique improvements.

Other Topics

I have deliberately omitted several other components of interviewing. These are:

- *Answering Competency Questions* – These are specific to each interviewee and each interview. You should already be well versed in how to answer these.
- *Responses to Common Questions* – Interviewers have a lot of pet questions, and there are a lot of questions that come up time and again in the normal course of interviews. There are many resources available on the Web to help you with these, so it would be redundant for me to include them here.
- *Handling Specific Objections* – Interviewers can have any number of concerns. There are too many to be addressed here. My strong recommendation is to anticipate them as much as you can and prepare effective responses before the interview instead of trying to improvise in the interview.
- *Salary Negotiation* – This is an extremely complex topic that could fill several books. The best thing that you can do is that if you are being represented by a competent external recruiter in whom you have confidence, then let the recruiter handle the negotiation. It always goes much better through an intermediary. For an example, think of how purchases are negotiated in residential real estate.

A Final Word

I would like to emphasize one important point about interviewing in case it isn't already clear to you. You don't have to be perfect at interviewing to get the job. Interviews are graded on a curve, so you only need to interview better than your competitors. If you are the best interviewee and meet the minimum qualifications stipulated by the company, you will be the one who gets the offer even if you don't do everything exactly as I have advised in this guide. So, implement as much of the advice contained here as you are able without worrying about the parts that are beyond you. Do this even if you don't think you have any talent for sales. Without a doubt, you will see a payoff for your efforts.

Your Feedback

My goal in this guide was to give you an introduction to the most important skills that you could use in selling yourself in an interview. While selling is a complex skill that can take a lifetime to master, the basics are pretty straightforward. I have selected those skills that will have the greatest benefit to you while also being relatively easy to learn and incorporate into your interviews. I have also tried to give you advice that you can't get elsewhere. I hope I have accomplished these objectives, and I would like to know whether or not I have done so. Therefore, if you have the time, I would welcome your feedback and war stories on how this guide has or has not helped you in your interviews. My email address is "fenyves@yahoo.com." It would also help me if you could make the subject of your email "Feedback on How to Sell Yourself in an Interview." I can then set up a filter to keep your message from inadvertently ending up in my spam folder.

Good luck on your interviews!

Also, remember the ABC of selling: Always Be Closing!

Part 2

Further Advice on Interviewing

5. Example Interview Questions You Can Ask

In this section, I have included a list of example questions to help you prepare your list of questions for each interview. You should note that very few of these questions can be answered in one word. As I stated earlier, one of your goals as you interview is to get the interviewer to do most of the talking. These mostly open-ended discovery questions will help you achieve this.

Questions About the Interviewer

When you schedule an interview with a potential employer, ask for the name and the position or title of each of the people you will be meeting. If you are given their names, research each of the interviewers on LinkedIn and via Google. First, you should review their LinkedIn profiles. In fact, you should print out their profiles and study them just as they should be studying your resume before the interview. Second, examine their web presence for any useful information. Look for anything that you might have in common with the person; e.g., college attended, companies or industries worked in, professional connections, group memberships, personal interests, etc. Make note of anything that might help you build rapport with the person. If you don't have any information prior to the interview, you will just have to wing it.

If you have acquaintances in common, ask the acquaintances about the person. You can even ask the other interviewers about the people you will be meeting next. This strategy works especially well in late-stage interviews. For example, if you are preparing to meet a high-level executive as the last step before an offer, you should ask your prospective boss and any future co-workers with whom you feel particularly good rapport for what to expect from the executive and any advice on how to succeed in the interview with the person. They will most likely help you because they will want you to succeed almost as much as you do. Remember, they have probably made up their minds to hire you. So, they would be almost as disappointed as you if the executive rejected you. At minimum, they don't want you to do badly because, if you blow the interview, it will reflect poorly on them for having recommended you to the executive.

Once your initial research is complete, prepare a list of questions for each interviewer. You may be able to use the same list, perhaps with some variations, for most of the people you meet.

- How long have you been with the company?
- [If he or she has been there six months or longer] What have you liked about working here?
- [If new to the company] What attracted you to the company and what have you found positive since you have been here?
- What qualities do successful people in the company/department have in common?
- What does a new person have to adjust to after they join?
- What can they do to ensure that they get off to a good start with the company?

- What do you look for in the people that are hired to work for you?
- What do you do to help a person get off to a successful start?
- What sort of feedback and review mechanism do you use to keep a person on the right track?
- Do you perceive that you have a management style? If so, what is it?
- What do you see as the major challenges in your position?
- If I were hired, what help would you want from me to meet these challenges?
- What can your subordinates do to make your job easier?

Questions About the Company

Assuming you've researched the company thoroughly, you should have answers to most of the following questions before the interview. In this case, you can use the interview to confirm the information that you've found and/or to fill in any blanks.

- What are the company's products, services, and target markets?
- What has been its history (especially if it is a relatively new company)?
- Where does it fit into the marketplace?
- Who are its top competitors?
- What are the challenges posed by the competition?
- What is the plan for overcoming these challenges?
- What are the company's advantages relative to the competition?
- What are the company's corporate goals?
- How does it plan to meet these goals?
- What sets the company apart as a place of employment; i.e., what makes it a good place to work?
- Can tell you tell me about something that happened here that wouldn't happen anywhere else?

Questions About the Department or Project

- What is the department's or project's primary mission or objective?
- Where does it fit into the overall scheme of the company?
- How is it organized; e.g., staff size, reporting structure, and division of responsibilities?
- If a high-tech job, what is the technical environment; e.g., platforms, languages, frameworks, latest technologies, development tools, etc.?
- What are the group's short-term (6-12 month) objectives?
- How well are these objectives being met?
    - If the objectives are being met, what is contributing to success?
    - If not being met, what are the challenges and the plans to overcome them?
- What is being done to ensure that the objectives are met?
- What are the key challenges that the group is facing currently?
- What is planned after the short-term goals are achieved?

Questions About the Position

- If I were hired, what is the most immediate thing that I could do to help the group meet its objectives?
- What do you expect me to accomplish in the first six months?
- What do you feel makes this an attractive position?
- What would be the most important thing that a person needs to be aware of to adjust successfully to this environment or position?
- What would be a list of possible assignments after the initial six months?
- If I performed satisfactorily, what sort of long-term advancement or recognition could I expect?
- What are the key skills that one would have to possess to be successful in this position?

If the position involves developing a new product that is sold on the market, the following make good additional or alternative questions:

- What needs and markets is the product intended to address?
- How well does it do so?
- Who are the chief competitors?
- What are the company's advantages against these competitors?
- What are the challenges it faces from the competition?
- How is it meeting these challenges?
- Where is the product in the current release cycle?
- What needs to be done to meet the next release date?
- What does the company expect of its employees to ensure it meets its release dates?
- What new technologies is the company adding to the product to stay competitive in the market?

6. Example Preinterview Plans

Chapter 4, Controlling the Interview, provides instruction on how to prepare for an interview. In this chapter, I'm including two real-world examples of how this advice can be put into practice. Both are my personal interview preparations for a part-time consulting position. The first is my outline for the initial phone interview with the hiring manager. The second is my plan for my subsequent meeting with him. Both are the actual documents I used with some minor changes to protect the privacy of the interviewer.

Background

Prior to my retirement, I did quite a bit of thinking about how I would fill my schedule once I was freed from the daily demands of a full-time job. High on the list of my planned activities was time spent advising people on how to find a job. After I stopped work, I started exploring ways to accomplish this.

One natural fit for my skills is in the outplacement industry. Outplacement firms are hired by corporations to help their laid-off workers find new jobs.

By searching the web, I identified RGH, a large outplacement firm with offices in the San Francisco Bay Area, to target for a part-time consulting position. A further search of LinkedIn uncovered that one of my connections was an outplacement consultant at RGH. I contacted her directly and explained my situation and goals. She was very friendly and receptive, and she forwarded my introductory email to Ron Baker, the local manager. Ron and I exchanged emails and scheduled a time for an initial phone interview. This led to an in-person interview and an offer of a part-time consulting position with RGH. The two examples in this chapter are my preparations for speaking with Ron.

Comments on the Preinterview Plans

Interview preparation takes time and effort.

As you can see from length of the two examples, I spent several hours putting them together. In addition, I invested around three hours researching the company and the interviewer. Such thorough preparation is an essential part of successfully selling yourself in an interview. Top salespeople are always better prepared than the customer which, in this case, is the interviewer. My outline for the phone interview, including research time, was about five hours. Because my call was going to be with the hiring manager directly, this time investment was worth it. If you are scheduled for a phone interview with a low-level HR person, I would not recommend this much effort.

My interview plan for the face-to-face meeting was an extension of the one for the phone interview with some overlap between the two. It only took a couple of hours to prepare.

Since this was my first job interview in forty years, I had to spend more time than if I had already had several interviews recently because I had to lay a lot of groundwork that only needs to be done once in each job search cycle. Nevertheless, other things being equal, the army that prepares best is the one that usually wins the battle. Therefore, I would like to reinforce with you the need to invest in the necessary preparation for each interview even if you don't think you have the time or don't feel you need to do so.

I had clear objectives for each interview.

As you can see, I had multiple specific objectives for each interview. I did not share my entire list with Ron, mostly because I did not need to. Nor would it have been advisable to tell him everything that was on my mind. However, I kept my objectives in focus during each interview and made certain that I achieved them. In the end, I succeeded in reaching all of them.

I would like to underline the really important point that you must know what you want out of each interview. This will help you stay on the right path during what is a very stressful encounter. In addition, once you have reached your objectives, you know that it is time for you to leave.

I prepared extensive lists of questions for each interview and organized them in a logical order.

Please take note of the large number of questions I prepared prior to each interview and that they were organized in a logical rather than random sequence. Most of these were conceived specifically for these interviews based on my research and my prior knowledge of the outplacement industry. However, the "Additional Questions" section of the on-site interview prep is lifted directly from Chapter 5 of this guide. There is no reason for you to reinvent the wheel either.

Closing at Each Interview

Consistent with my strong emphasis on closing, at the end of the phone interview I asked for a face-to-face meeting with Ron and set up a date and time for this while we were still on the phone. This ensured that seeing me did not fall off his priority list.

At the in-person interview, I asked Ron as we were wrapping up "Do you think we have a deal here?" He laughed and replied, "I can see that you are definitely a salesman. Yes, we have a deal." There are two points I would like to draw your attention to in this exchange. First, by closing, I cemented the job offer. Second, even though Ron could plainly see that he was being closed, he was not put off by my directness. Therefore, I would like to reinforce my prior advice to you – Always Be Closing.

Interview Plan for Call with Ron Baker of RGH

Introduction

- I noticed from your LinkedIn profile that you relatively recently moved to Northern California.
- What motivated you to make the change?
- From what I've seen, most people either prefer Northern California or Southern California but not both. How do you like it here?
- I'm from Toronto, so I love it here.
- What would you like to accomplish on today's phone call?

My Objectives

1. Assess their staffing needs.
2. Understand what is involved and required for any appropriate open positions.
3. Understand their hiring process.
4. Get agreement to move to the next step.

Questions for Ron

1. What is the size and scope of RGH's operations in the Bay Area:
   a. Number and location of offices?
   b. Number of employees and consultants working out of each?
   c. Geographic area served?
2. What types of services does RGH offer to corporations from the Bay Area offices? RGH's web site lists:
   a. Career transition and outplacement.
   b. Finding and attracting talent.
   c. Career development programs.
   d. Organizational restructuring.
   e. Workforce transformation and organizational change.
3. How is business given that the unemployment rate is so low?
4. What services and programs does the RGH offer to laid off workers?
5. How many people take advantage of these in a typical year or month?
6. What is the format for delivering services to job seekers:
   a. One-on-one coaching
   b. Group lectures
   c. Discussion groups
   d. Videoconferencing
   e. Telephone consultation, etc.
   f. Web resources
7. How do you organize the services you provide laid off workers:
   a. Assign a single consultant or a team?

8. Who are the staff that deliver these programs?
    a. Are they salaried, full-time consultants or part-time consultants?
    b. What are their backgrounds?
9. What activities do your staff perform with each laid off worker?
    a. Do your consultants specialize; e.g., resume writing only or interviewing only?
    b. Or are they expected to provide a complete job hunting assistance that includes everything?
10. What you look for the people you hire?
11. What are your expectations of your consultants?
12. How will you and I know whether or not I'm doing a good job?

My Relevant Skills

- Interview coaching.
- Salary negotiation.
- Resume writing.
- Job search process.
- Post-interview analysis.
- Pep talks (effective listening, counseling).
- Having been a hiring manager, I can advise on what qualities managers are looking for.

My goals are simple:

- Engage in an activity that I enjoy and I am good at.
- Make a contribution that is valuable and valued.
- Job parameters that fit my life: limited hours, limited commute, and congenial people.
- Work that I can leave behind at the office.

Possible Objection

Having been my own boss for 32 years, can I be managed?

- How serious a concern is this?
- The fact that I was my own boss is actually an advantage because it shows that I am self-directed and do not need supervision.

Interview Plan for Meeting with Ron Baker of RGH

Ron's Objectives?

- What would you like to accomplish in today's meeting?
- Do you have any pressing topics/questions you'd like to cover before we start?

My Objectives

1. Confirm which is the most appropriate position for me.
2. Understand what day-to-day job activities in the job.
3. Understand what Ron's expectations are of his staff.
4. Understand the hiring process.
5. Get agreement to move to the next step with Ron.
6. Set up a meeting/call with Silicon Valley general manager or at least a recommendation from Ron to do so.

Questions for Ron

1. Can you please paint me a more detailed picture of how you deliver your services to job seekers (What per cent of the process does each constitute?):
   a. One-on-one coaching
   b. Web resources
   c. Group lectures
   d. Discussion groups
   e. Videoconferencing
   f. Telephone consultation, etc.
2. Detailed questions about the position:
   a. Can you describe a typical week for a consultant?
   b. How are the appointments scheduled; e.g., candidates sign up online, scheduler makes appointments, counselors set up sessions directly with candidates?
   c. What happens in the typical counseling session?
   d. What materials are available to the counselor to use in each session; e.g., interview guides, sources of job leads, video recording of mock interviews, etc.
   e. How are counselors and candidates matched up?
   f. How are new counselors trained and brought up to speed?
   g. How are counselors evaluated?
   h. What are the best parts of the job?
   i. What are the challenges?
3. What do you look for in the people that are hired to work for you? My notes from our phone call say you are looking for people who:
   a. Understand the marketplace.
   b. Have a desire and an attitude to help others.

   c. Are highly productive and focus on results.
 4. What are your expectations of your consultants; i.e., how will you and I know whether or not I'm doing a good job?

My Relevant Skills

- Interview coaching.
- Salary negotiation.
- Job search process.
- Post-interview analysis.
- Pep talks (effective listening, counseling).
- Having been a hiring manager, I can advise on what qualities managers are looking for.
- Resume writing.

My goals are simple:

- Engage in an activity that I enjoy and I am good at.
- Make a contribution that is valuable and valued.
- Job parameters that fit my life: limited hours, limited commute, and congenial people.
- Work that I can leave behind at the office.

Additional Questions

Questions About Ron and his Team

- What qualities do successful people in your team have in common?
- What does a new person have to adjust to after they join?
- What can I do to ensure that I get off to a good start with the company?
- What do you do to help a person get off to a successful start; e.g., training, coaching, feedback?
- What sort of feedback and review mechanism do you use to keep a person on the right track?
- What do you see as the major challenges in your position?
- If I were hired, what help would you want from me to meet these challenges?
- What can your subordinates do to make your job easier?

Questions About the Department or Project

- How is your group's performance measured?
- How well are these objectives being met?
- What are the keys to this success?
- What are the key challenges that are facing the group at this time?

- If I were hired, what is the most immediate thing that I could do to help you meet your objectives?
- What do you expect me to accomplish in the first six months?
- What do you feel makes this an attractive position?
- What would be the most important thing that a person needs to be aware of in order to adjust successfully to this environment or position?

Possible Objection

Having been my own boss for 32 years, can I be managed?

- How serious a concern is this?
- The fact that I was my own boss is actually an advantage because it shows that I am self-directed and do not need supervision. \

7. Translating Your Features Into Related Benefits

If you feel comfortable with the advice in the main section of this guide, one of the ways you can take your interview preparation to the next level is by thinking more deeply about what makes you a good employee.

To reiterate, you are the product that you are selling. Products have features. These features provide something of value to the customer; i.e., benefits. Customers *don't buy features* (even if this is not immediately obvious). Customers *buy the benefits* the features provide. For example:

Tesla is an electric car, but people don't buy the feature that it's electric. They buy the benefits of electric operation:

- Reduced operating costs
- Social benefit of reduced pollution
- Permission to drive in the commuter lane
- Silent operation
- Impress friends and neighbors

In the same way you can translate your features into benefits; i.e., how your feature (skill, knowledge, experience) can help the prospective employer:

- Feature: you are intelligent.
- Benefit: you can learn new information and skills quickly, master complex material, and solve tough problems, etc.

- Feature: you can think creatively.
- Benefit: you can help your employer adapt to changing environments.

- Feature: you can work collaboratively.
- Benefit: you can fit in well with the existing team and can move easily to new roles within the company.

- Feature: you can lead teams.
- Benefit: you can get maximum results from the people who need to work together to achieve a desired result.

- Feature: you work hard.
- Benefit: you can apply yourself to deliver both high quality and high quantity output.

- Feature: you are disciplined and determined.
- Benefit: you will persevere when faced with a daunting challenge.

Remember: It's not enough to make claims as in the above bullets. You need to have concrete examples from your past that prove your statements.

8. Responding to the Salary Question

"How much money do you want?"

You will be asked this question or its equivalent at various points in the interview cycle. At the end of the cycle, this is a negotiation question. At the beginning or in the middle of the cycle it is a qualification question that is used primarily to filter out candidates. In either situation, it is a question that you should handle with care and skill lest your answer proves costly to you.

Regardless of at what stage in the hiring process you are asked this question, you want to respond with a non-numerical answer; i.e., don't quote any numbers, not even ranges.

The reason for not quoting a specific number is that, unless you can read minds, your stated number will be either higher or lower than the salary the company was hoping to offer to the person hired. If your stated expectation is above their target, there is a good chance you will be eliminated from consideration. If your number is below their budget and they hire you, you are likely to receive an offer less than you could have gotten otherwise. The lost potential income could amount to tens of thousands of dollars, or even more, over your working life.

In addition, if your salary guess is significantly lower than their estimation of your worth, they may assume that you have some serious hidden defects that reduce your dollar value in your mind. Rather than taking a risk on hiring a flawed candidate like you at a bargain salary, they are likely to rule you out.

Quoting a range doesn't eliminate the problems I just stated because there is a risk that they will latch on to either the lower or higher number in your range as the salary you expect. Now you are back in the same situation as if you had quoted just a single number.

There are two techniques for replying to the question that avoid the problems just discussed:

1. Answer directly but don't give out any specific numbers or ranges.
2. Answer the question with another question.

Responding Directly

Below is an example of how recommend you reply to this question the first time that it is asked. There are two components to the answer. First, tell the interviewer that you are interested in the position and why. Then give an answer that sounds good but does not commit you to any specific number or range. On most occasions, such an answer will satisfy the interviewer. Here is an example of how you could respond:

"I honestly cannot give you a specific number or range at this time, mostly because I haven't given salary any thought yet. My number one goal is to find a position that is a good match for my skills, one where I could be successful and one where I would be happy for the long term. So, salary is of secondary concern to me.

Therefore, rather than giving you any hastily-conceived numbers, I would like to leave you with the thought that I'm very interested in this position. I think it is a job that is a very good match for my skills and career objectives. I think I could make a valuable contribution to your company, and I think I would really enjoy working here. So, I would like to rely on your honesty and integrity to make me the best offer that you can which is both fair within your internal salary structure and competitive in the marketplace. Do you think that is something you could do?"

The two key phrases in this answer are "fair within your salary structure" and "competitive in the marketplace." This response puts two points of pressure on the interviewer. First, they will have to pay you enough to compete with any other offers you may receive. Second, it makes it difficult for them to give you a pay package that is much lower than what they are already paying others in similar positions at the company. It also puts the burden on the employer rather than on you to figure out what offer would meet these criteria.

Most of the time such an answer will suffice. The typical interviewer will feel uncomfortable pressing you hard for an answer. However, occasionally you will come across a tough negotiator, usually an internal recruiter, who will push you very hard for a specific number. The way I recommend you deal with such a person is to keep answering their questions with additional questions. Below is an example of this approach.

Incidentally, if you get asked the salary question in a phone screen, you can use the non-numerical response above, but you'll have to modify it slightly to take into account that you don't know anything yet about the job or the company.

Answering with a Question

Use the strategy of responding to probing questions about salary by replying with a question that puts the pressure back on the interviewer. Picking up from the example above, here is how this dialog might go:

Interviewer: "I like your attitude about salary, but I need to have a specific number from you. How much money do you want?"

You: "As I said, I'm not really sure what that number might be because I haven't done any market research, plus I don't know your internal salary structure. What is the salary range for this position?"

Interviewer: "$120,000 to $180,000 per year. Would you accept that?"

You: "What part of that range do you think would be correct for me based on my skills relative to others in the group?"

Interviewer: "I'm thinking no more than $150,000. Would you take that?"

You: "Do you think that would be fair internally?"

Interviewer: "I will verify that, but I believe it is. Would you accept?"

You: "Do you think that would be your best offer?"

Interviewer: "Yes, I can't see being able to offer you more than that. Would you take it?"

You: "Well, if that is your best offer, then please make me that offer because I want to work here. What do we need to do to formalize the offer?"

As you can see from the above, you gave absolutely no numbers and made the interviewer do all the work. Now $150,000 a year may or may not be acceptable to you. If it is, then you can just take it. If not, then you can try to negotiate better terms once you have a written offer. Again, this document is not meant to be a negotiation guide, and very few discussions would go exactly as I just described. However, I want to leave you with the principle that you should never, ever be the one to throw out the first real salary number. Make the interviewer come up with a proposal first. The best way to do this is to keep replying with questions.

"What is your current compensation?"

Interviewers will also ask you information about your current compensation. Try not to give this information out, if possible. Before you give a direct answer, try the following:

You: "What is the salary range for the position?"

Interviewer: "$120,000 to $180,000 per year."

You: "My income falls within that range so we should not have a problem."

Few people will accept this response, but it's worth a try.

If the interviewer insists on knowing your current compensation, then you should answer truthfully, assuming two things. First, your compensation is in line with market norms. Second, you're not looking for a raise greater than 10% nor willing to take a cut greater than 5%. As you answer, state your base salary and any guaranteed cash incentives, bonuses or other payments that show up on your W-2. Do not include fringe benefits such as medical plans, retirement contributions, pre-IPO stock options, 401K contributions, etc. You may mention these, but clearly identify them as separate from your base compensation.

If you are looking for a salary increase of more than 10% or are willing to take a pay cut of greater than 5%, then do everything possible not to reveal your current compensation. This is a very difficult thing to do, and how you would accomplish this would vary from situation to situation. So, you should get some expert advice specific to your needs.

The reason for not revealing your current salary in situations where you are looking for a large increase or willing to take a pay cut is because this is not the norm. Contrary to what many may have heard, most people change jobs for a salary that is about the same or not more than 10% above their current one. So, your anomalous situation is highly likely to cause concerns in the mind of the interviewer. There is no one right answer for dealing with such a situation. So, again, get professional advice, usually from a skilled recruiter, and not from your friends.

9. Handling Frequently Asked Tricky Questions

Four Tricky Questions

The four questions below have two things in common. First, they come up in a high percentage of interviews. Second, the wrong answer to any one of them can easily drop you from consideration. Interviewers don't ask these questions to identify the right candidate. Instead, they use them to weed out people to reduce the candidate pool. There is no perfect answer to any of these questions that will clinch you the offer. However, there are many wrong answers, any of which could get you instantly disqualified. To avoid being eliminated, your strategy in responding to these questions should be to treat each as a landmine that you have to deftly side-step in such a way that you avoid the trap without seeming to be evasive.

It is essential that you formulate and rehearse at least one effective answer to each of these four questions because you do not want to miss out on a good job offer simply because you were unprepared. Test out each of your answers on friends before you use them in interviews to confirm that you are on the right track.

Although you will rehearse your answers, make sure that you sound spontaneous in your delivery instead of stilted like a robot. One way to do this is to pause after the question is asked as if you were thinking about the question and how you should reply. You can even insert some hesitant throat clearing as if you were trying to buy time. Then, as you answer, don't rattle off your response. Instead, hem and haw a bit to make it seem as if you were searching for the right words. This is obviously fake to you, but you want to be so well rehearsed that you seem natural and spontaneous to the interviewer. Again, practice on your friends until you get it right.

1. "What are your weaknesses?"

Interviewers ask this question all the time without realizing how rude and stupid it is. Regarding the point about rudeness, can you picture an interviewee ever asking the question, "What makes this company a lousy place to work?" Personally, I can't imagine any interviewer not being offended by such a question. Yet companies think nothing of asking the same question in reverse of a candidate.

As for why the question is stupid, there is no value in asking the question because only the most inexperienced interviewee would ever give an honest answer. They are basically asking the salesperson, the interviewee in this case, to criticize their product. You would never think to ask a car salesperson "Can you tell me all the reasons why I shouldn't buy your car?" because you know you would not get a straight answer. No successful salesperson would ever dream of criticizing their product. In the same way, you should never, ever criticize yourself in an interview.

While it could be very satisfying for you to point out these problems with the question to an interviewer, doing so will not get you the offer. So, you have to play the game and give a response that seems to give a direct answer to the question without revealing any of your real weaknesses.

The best answer you can give is to say that you have no weaknesses *relative to the position.* The key phrase in your answer will be "relative to the position" because there are no perfect candidates. Everyone has some shortcomings. However, a characteristic that might be a weakness for one position might, in fact, be a strength in a different one. For example, "I hate to sit at a computer all day" would be a weakness in a position, such as software engineer, that requires pounding on a keyboard most of the time. However, this could be a strength in a different position, such as outside sales, in which you want the person to be in front of customers instead of hiding behind a computer screen.

Here is how you could construct a response using this strategy:

"Based on my analysis of the position plus the information I have obtained through my interviews with your company, I believe I would bring the following strengths to the job. (State the top 3-5 strongest attributes that qualify you for the position.) Therefore, I think I could do a really good job here. So, I don't perceive that I have any weaknesses *relative to the position.* Wouldn't you agree with my assessment?"

Note the tie-down question tacked on to the end.

Such a response will satisfy most interviewers. However, occasionally you will run into an interviewer who, for whatever reason, will persist in digging for weaknesses. If you find yourself in front of such a person, you can try *one* of the following approaches. Use whichever you are most comfortable with or think would work best in the particular case.

- Use a porcupine question to make the interviewer come up with a weakness. Here is what you might say, "You seem very intent on uncovering a weakness in me. Is this because you perceive that I have one? If so, what is your concern?" By responding with a question, you will force the interviewer to reveal any concerns they may have and thus give yourself an opportunity to overcome them.
- Give an example of a trait that is actually a strength for the job in question and one that could not be misconstrued as a failing. For example, "I would never be good in sales because I could never lie to people just to get them to buy a product that I didn't believe in." This is usually safe because most individuals have an aversion to sales people. Obviously, you don't want to say this when you are applying for a sales job. In such a case, you could reply with "I could never be happy in a job where I spent 100% of my time looking at a computer screen with no people interaction all day."
- Give a response that essentially says that you have no weaknesses, only areas for personal growth; e.g., When interviewing for a management, not an executive, opening, you could say "Obviously, I'm not ready to take on a VP-level position,

but I am highly motivated by challenges and opportunities for personal growth. So, I will work as hard as necessary to succeed in the immediate position and to develop the skills to take on additional responsibilities."

- State something that would be an immediate deal breaker for you in any position regardless of the offer the company made you; e.g., an expectation that you respond to emails and text messages 24x7, including 3:00 am on Sunday. However, you should state this in a diplomatic way such as, "I could never succeed in a job that required me to constantly handle crises in the middle of the night. I am very willing to work extra hard, but I do need uninterrupted sleep to recharge and replenish myself for work the next day. How many times a week or month would I have to handle something in the middle of the night?" The question at the end of this example is a form of porcupine question that allows you to reassert control of the interview and steer the conversation away from your possible shortcomings to a different topic, ideally one that you have chosen.

One word of caution, be careful that you don't state something that could be interpreted in a negative way. For example, if you were to say, "I work too hard," some people might interpret that as a positive. However, others may conclude that the reason you work 60 hours a week is that you are not very good at your job, and it takes you 60 hours to accomplish what others could get done in 40 hours. Similarly, a statement that "I am too honest" could cause people to infer that you are blunt, opinionated and difficult to get along with. So, tread carefully.

2. "Give me an example of when you failed."

This question is similar to the previous one in that it asks you to point out your flaws. It too is rude because the word "failed" is highly prejudicial and implies that you are a flawed candidate.

Regardless of how you feel about the question, you will have to provide an answer that will satisfy the interviewer. Here are some suggestions for handling the question:

- Do not, under any circumstances, admit to any failures (or failings.)
- Try to deflect the question by using the porcupine technique. "I can't think of any failures off the top of my head. What information are you trying to learn by asking this question? If you can give me some clarification, maybe I can provide you the information you need a different way."
- Reframe the question by talking not about "failure" but about "valuable lessons" you learned, or about "setbacks" or "disappointments" you may have experienced.
- An excellent example of the "valuable lessons" tactic is to describe a project or a startup you were a part of that was unsuccessful. Then explain how the experience allowed you to gain some new skill or knowledge that helped you succeed in your next career step. Craft your answer in such a way that you appear completely blameless for the lack of success.
- As an overall principle, never give an answer that can be interpreted as evidence

that you are a flawed candidate. Also, never give an answer that is completely self-revealing, but at the same time, make sure you don't sound evasive either.

A variation of this question about failure is "Give me an example of a lesson you have learned from making a mistake. What did you do differently going forward?" This is actually a pretty good question, provided the candidate gives a completely honest answer. So, do not fall into the trap of giving a fully-revealing response. The same advice applies to this question as to the previous one; do not say anything that could make you seem defective in any way. A couple of ways you can avoid falling into this trap are as follows:

- Give an example from early in your career where you suffered a painful lesson because you were too inexperienced to know better. A good example would be where you put your trust in someone or something and they betrayed that trust. Then talk about how you learned to be much more cautious and skeptical and careful in the future.
- Instead of talking about a mistake you made, talk about a calculated risk you took which didn't work out; e.g., you went with a startup that didn't succeed but was a good learning opportunity. Make sure, though, that in no way could you be blamed for the startup's lack of success or for using poor judgment in accepting a job with it.

3. "Where do you want to be in three (or five, or ten) years?"

The reason this question is tricky is that, unless you know the interviewer very well, you have no idea what answer would satisfy them. You don't want to scare the interviewer by being overly ambitious or too specific in your goals. On the other hand, you don't want to seem unmotivated and lacking ambition. So, you need to walk a fine line.

The following are definitely *poor* answers:

- You have no goals.
- Stating poorly thought-out or contradictory goals.
- Giving overly-specific or overly-ambitious goals.
- Saying that you want to run your own company. The interviewer is looking for an employee, not the CEO of a startup.

The best way to answer this question is to do what politicians do. Give an answer full of generalizations that sound good without saying anything of substance that can get you rejected. Here is an example of an answer that I often advise candidates use when applying for a high-tech job:

"Three (or five, or ten) years are a long time in high tech, so I don't know exactly where I will be. However, I do know that I want the following:

- I want to be working for a company that I believe in and one that is succeeding in its business.

- I want to feel that I am making an important contribution to the product or project on which I am working.
- I want to be in a position where I will continue to grow both personally and professionally.
- I want to be challenged and stimulated but not overwhelmed.
- I want to be working with compatible colleagues who share my passion and commitment to the success of whatever endeavor we are in.
- I want to have a position of responsibility where the responsibility is in line with my abilities.
- I want compensation and recognition that fairly and appropriately recognizes my contributions.
- I want to keep up with the technical advances in my area of expertise."

The value of an answer like the preceding is that there is nothing in it that should rule you out as a candidate while at the same time it sounds substantive and well thought-out. Best of all, this answer would be true for most people. It should satisfy most interviewers.

If the interviewer follows up with a question that tries to pin you down to specifics, such as "Do you want to be in management?," don't fall into the trap of giving a yes or no answer. Instead, once again do what politicians do; answer "That depends." Here's one way you could do this. "While I have thought about a management career path, at this point I know I'm not ready to step into a management role. So, I would like to keep that question open. Why don't we see how I do in the position for which you are hiring me? If I demonstrate an aptitude and a readiness for management, then we can discuss a possible promotion when a management opportunity opens up."

4. "Tell me about yourself."

This is a very common question and usually indicates that the interviewer has not prepared well for the interview. So, the question is a strong signal to you that you should have an easy time controlling this interview once you get past it. What makes this question tricky is that it is so vague and open-ended that it is hard for you to know what information the interviewer is looking for. Therefore, before you launch into an answer, try a porcupine question. "Given that I have a lot of experience, there is a lot to tell. If you could pinpoint what part of my resume or experience was of the greatest interest to you, I can focus on that?" If the person gives you a specific answer, you can direct the conversation to that topic and may not even need to give a direct response to the "Tell me about yourself" question.

If the interviewer insists that you talk about yourself, then you should be prepared with a short (maximum two-minute) response as below. Under no circumstances should you give a lengthy speech. Even five minutes would be much too long.

In replying, don't rehash the contents of your resume nor recite your biography. Instead, imagine that the question was "Why should I hire you?" or "What makes you a good fit for this job?" Of course, you don't let the interviewer know that this is what you are doing.

Your answer should adhere to the following structure:

- A headline sentence that summarizes you as a professional in a way that relates to the position for which you are being interviewed; e.g., "I am a highly experienced CFO with extensive experience in the healthcare field."
- A *brief* narrative that incorporates 3-5 of your features and benefits that are most relevant to the position for which you are applying (refer to Chapter 7.)
- A general statement of your career goals. It should be brief, non-specific, and relevant to the position at hand; e.g., "At this point I am looking for a senior level position in Finance with a promising company that can benefit from my skills and expertise."
- A tie-down question at the end; e.g., "Does that quick summary give you an adequate overview of who I am?"

Notice how the question at the end allows you to reassert your control of the interview. Remember, the person doing the questioning is the one in charge.

Other Standard Interview Questions

Below is a list of questions that routinely come up in interviews. The common element among them is that they all ask for an essay-type answer rather than a short response. I'm including them here so that you will have a chance to think about how you would answer each if asked. By giving some thought to these questions ahead of time, you'll be less likely to give an answer that will get you eliminated.

- How would your supervisor describe you? What about your coworkers?
- How would you describe the ideal working environment?
- How do you deal with criticism from your manager? How about from coworkers?
- What did you most enjoy about your last job?
- What did you think of your previous manager?
- What can you offer us that other people cannot?
- What about this job attracts you? What is there about it that is less than desirable for you?
- Give me a specific example project that you were responsible for organizing from beginning to end. How did you go about it?
- Give me an example of a difficult problem you solved at work and describe how you went about solving it.
- Can you describe for me your top three professional accomplishments? What makes these special for you?
- What is the difference between activity and results? Can you give me some examples of each from your past?
- What is the one thing in your life that you have not been able to accomplish or complete that gives you the most frustration or disappointment? Why didn't you

complete it?
- What is the riskiest thing you have ever done? Why was it risky? Why did you choose to take a chance, and how did things turn out?
- What do you consider the most effective way to influence someone to a particular point of view?

Obviously, there are hundreds of other questions interviewers ask beyond these examples, so I won't try for a comprehensive list. My main goal is to encourage you to think about how you would answer these specific questions and also to practice the generalized technique for handling other such questions.

Your standard approach to answering an essay question like the ones above should be as follows:

- Ask a clarifying question, if necessary, to ensure that you understand what is being asked.
- Consider several possible responses, not just the first thing that comes into your head.
- Evaluate the merits of each response for the specific interview.
- Select the most appropriate answer.
- Articulate your answer in a way that presents you in the best light.

Clearly the foregoing steps require a lot of time and careful thought, more time than is available in the heat of an interview. That is why pre-interview preparation is so important and why I'm including this chapter in this guide.

10. Support Statements and Active Listening

Support Statements and Active Listening are two techniques that skilled salespeople use to build rapport and help close sales. The two techniques are related but different in construction and application.

Support Statement

A Support Statement is a technique used in sales to reinforce something the prospective customer says which is helpful to your making the sale. The two best opportunities for using a Support Statement are when the interviewer either:

1. Compliments your product, or
2. States that a benefit that your product provides is important to them.

A Support Statement is delivered as follows:

- Step 1 – Agree with what the prospect just said. Here are two example Support Statements:
    - "You are absolutely correct, reducing finished goods inventory to the minimum is a key component of maintaining profit margins."
    - "You are right, my management of the Webcor IPO was a model of how it should be done."
- Step 2 – Expand on the statement, if appropriate; e.g.,
    - In the first example above, "Tight control of the supply chain is one main way of controlling finished goods inventory and is one of my strengths."
    - Or in the second example above, "The key to my success in the IPO was my understanding of and close relationship with the major players on Wall Street."

A key reason Support Statements are so effective is that people can be skeptical of the things you say in an interview, but if they say it themselves they will believe it. So, if they say something that helps your case, make sure they remember it by letting them know how smart they were to say it.

A word of caution: use Support Statements judiciously. If you overuse the technique, you may come across as fawning and phony. Also, be careful not to agree with things that don't help you. In such a case, just stay silent and move on to the next topic.

Active Listening

Active Listening is a communication technique that increases understanding and rapport between speaker and listener. Rather than passively listening to the speaker (or not listening at all), the active listener pays close attention to both verbal and body language, then repeats back the most important points of the speaker's message.

Restating what you heard shows the speaker conclusively that you are paying attention to them and thus will quickly build trust and rapport.

Also, it is an almost perfect way to avoid misunderstandings. Since you repeat back a summary of what you heard, the speaker then has a chance to correct anything that you didn't understand. If you clear up a misunderstanding immediately, it won't have a chance to throw your interview off track.

The most obvious use of Active Listening is during the qualifying and answering objections stages. Here are some examples of Active Listening being used in interviews:

Responding to a Positive Statement

Here's how you use Active Listening where you hear something good about the opportunity:

Interviewer: "Sales have doubled in the last three years and are on track to do so again this year."

Instead of just smiling and nodding positively, use an Active Listening response: "That's exciting. Your rapid growth is amazing, and it reflects exactly the type of company I want to be a part of."

The structure of the Active Listening response above is:

1. State your positive emotion; i.e., "excitement".
2. Acknowledge the content of the interviewer's statement; i.e., "rapid growth".
3. Express your liking or interest in that aspect of the opportunity.

As a word of caution about Active Listening, be careful not to parrot the interviewer. If you do, your technique will become obvious and come off as phony. Instead of building rapport, you will create distrust. So, avoid repeating verbatim what they said. Instead, rephrase their statement using slightly different words as you reflect back to them your understanding of what you heard.

Responding to a Problem Statement

Here is an example of how you use Active Listening when the interviewer states a problem or need:

Interviewer: "The failures of our outsourced manufacturers have set back our ship dates badly."

Active Listening response: "Sounds like your manufacturers have let you down severely. When business partners fail to deliver, it can have serious consequences."

This statement is effective. However, when the interviewer states a problem that you can solve, this is a perfect opportunity for a Support Statement.

Instead of simply actively listening, use a Support Statement: "You're right. When business partners don't live up to their commitments, it can have serious consequences for your business. That is why we set up some very effective safeguards against such problems at my last employer. Would you like to hear about them?"

Now you have the perfect opportunity to talk about that aspect of your background and experience that is most relevant and of greatest interest to the interviewer.

Bottom Line

Don't be a passive listener. Use Active Listening to build rapport and to express your enthusiasm and interest in the opportunity. Use Support Statements as responses to statements of problems or needs by the interviewer where your skills and experience can help.

11. Advanced Closing Techniques

Tie-Down Questions

Tie-downs are questions which look for a "yes" answer from the interviewer. You ask these intermittently during the interview to cement, or "tie down," a fact, opinion or other item that is favorable to you. These minor "yes" answers help advance your candidacy towards a job offer. Tie-downs are another effective sales technique that I learned from the book "How to Master the Art of Selling" by Tom Hopkins. The questions themselves are easy to ask. What makes this an advanced technique is that it takes a lot of conscious effort and practice to remember to use tie-downs and to use them so that they sound natural and unforced. Here is what Hopkins says about the technique:

> When you work with a new prospect, don't you agree that you should try for several minor yeses before you go for the big yes that means they've bought? That makes sense, doesn't it?
>
> Certainly.
>
> Wouldn't it be helpful to have a reliable technique for starting a flow of minor yeses every time you work with possible buyers? That's what tie-downs do, don't they? And you're getting a little tired of all these questions, aren't you?
>
> That's why it's so important not to overuse tie-downs. They're extremely effective but, unless used sparingly, they grate on people.

Tie-down questions can take several forms such as being tagged onto the end of a sentence. They can also be stand-alone questions as illustrated in the advanced close below. There are multiple reasons why you want to use this technique and why it works:

- It takes a lot of effort to overcome the inertia of a locomotive standing still on a railway track. However, once it is rolling it will keep rolling unless a great deal of effort is exerted to stop it. In the same way, affirmative answers to your tie-down questions get the interviewer rolling down the track in the direction of making a decision in your favor. The more times they hear themselves saying "yes" to you during the interview, the more difficult it will be for them to say "no" at the end.
- If you get a "no" answer to a tie-down, you know you have a problem and can address it immediately rather than letting it linger hidden in the interviewer's mind where it can cause them to decide against you.
- The flow of minor yeses throughout the interview will make your asking for a commitment at the end of the interview seem like the natural and logical thing to do.

The easiest way for you to get started with this technique is to use it every time you have answered an interview question. Ask such tie-downs as:

"Did I answer your question correctly?"
"Did I understand your question correctly?"
"Is that the answer you were looking for?"
"Do you agree?"
"Is that correct?"

Below is a longer script illustrating the technique being used in a late-stage interview.

Example Advanced Close Using Tie-Downs

This long script is too daunting for an inexperienced interviewee to attempt and should not be delivered exactly as presented. It is simply meant to illustrate what is possible once you are adept and confident at closing. In real life, the points need to be made, but they should be woven more naturally into the end of the interview:

You: "Well, Mary, you, your colleagues and I have spent a lot of time getting to know each other. We have exchanged a lot of information and formed our opinions. Would you mind if I took a few moments to summarize where I think things stand?"

Mary: "Go ahead."

You: "At this point, I can definitively tell you that I want to work here because:

First, I think that railcar leasing is an exciting business with huge potential, so I feel it would be very stimulating to work here, and I can see myself staying here indefinitely. Everyone here seems very committed to being here over the long haul. So, my long-term attitude would fit right in with your values. Am I correct?"

Mary: "Yes, you are."

You: "Second, the CFO role makes use of my strengths so I'm confident that I can be successful in the position and, therefore, be a good hire and also be happy in the job.

Third, your planned IPO requires someone to come in and get a lot done in a hurry. I really enjoy that kind of challenge, and the IPO I ran for Webcor has given me direct experience that will help me get it done efficiently for you.

Also, several people I met told me that they liked the expertise I gained from my prior five years of CFO experience. They also commented that they were impressed by my answers to some very tough financial questions and by the fact that I could think on my feet. From this feedback, I am assuming that they think I can do the job. Is my assumption correct?"

Mary: "Yes, they all gave you the thumbs up."

You: "Do you also believe that I could do this job?"

Mary: "Yes, I do."

You: "They were especially eager for me to explain my role on the IPO because you need someone on staff to keep the investment bankers honest on their feet. Is this important to you as well?"

Mary: "Yes, it's critical."

You: "Do you think that you can rely on me to do that?"

Mary: "Yes, you have convinced me."

You: "From all this it sounds like we have a good match here, don't you think?"

Mary: "Yes, we do."

You: " Great! In that case, would you like to bring me on board?"

Mary: "Yes, I would."

You: "Wonderful! How do we make this come about?"

Notice how the series of minor yeses made it natural to use the assumptive close "How do we make this come about?" Also, after giving multiple yeses to the tie-down questions, it would be difficult for the interviewer to say "no" at the end when asked for a commitment, wouldn't you agree? This example illustrates why the tie-down question is one of my favorite closing aids.

However, it is still possible to get a 'no' after all the yeses to your tie-downs. A 'no' response indicates that the interviewer has an unresolved objection. Uncover it and handle it. Then close again.

To deliver an advanced close like the one above:

1. Say that you want the job and back up your statement with a few substantive reasons.
2. Summarize the top 2-5 reasons why you would make a good hire for the position.
3. Tie down each reason with a minor close.
4. If you get a "yes" to every minor close, go for a hard close and ask for a commitment.
5. If you get a "no" to a closing question, immediately uncover the interviewer's concern, handle it, and try closing again.

If you are unable to get a commitment after executing the above steps, either you have not satisfied the interviewer's stated concerns, or the person has a hidden concern. In either case, you should send out more resumes and go on more interviews because you are unlikely to receive an offer from this company.

Zero-to-Ten Close

The zero-to-ten close is a soft close that is relatively easy for anyone to try. But you will need to practice it before you try it in an interview.

Here is how the close goes:

"Now before we wrap up, I'm wondering if you could give me your assessment of our interview. Can you tell me on a zero to ten scale how you assess the fit? Zero would be absolutely no fit, and we just wasted an hour of each other's time. Ten would indicate we have a perfect match, and we should move forward to bring me on board as soon as possible.

I don't sense that this is a zero, but I'm not sure where I stand. What do you think?"

Some interviewers may decline to give you a rating. If they do refuse, then try some of the other closing techniques in Section 2. However, most people will give you a number or a range such as "between six and seven." If they give you two numbers, assume the score is the higher of the two numbers.

Here is how you could respond depending on the interviewer's rating:

Rating between 0 and 5

Unless the interviewer never gives anybody a score higher than six, you are not going to get this job. If you just plain don't like the interviewer, you can just get up and leave. However, if the person seems decent and sincere, try to get some feedback that would help you in future interviews.

"From the sound of it, you don't see a strong fit here. Am I correct? Just for my benefit, I wonder if you could explain why not?"

Rating of 6 or 7

This is a score, while not superb, is something you could possibly work with. So, try to move your case forward by asking the following:

"While not perfect, that seems like a respectable score. What things do you feel are the positives that I bring to the position?"

Listen and reinforce the positive comments. This is a perfect opportunity to use Support Statements.

"What do you feel is keeping the score from being an eight instead of a seven?"

The interviewer will probably list some concerns. Handle the concerns as discussed elsewhere in this guide. If you are successful in putting the concerns to rest, try closing again:

"Given that I seem to have answered your concerns, do you think the score should perhaps be an eight instead of a seven?"

If you get a positive response, then try for a hard close and a commitment to move to the next step.

Response of 8 or 9

Eight is usually about as high a score as you can get in an interview because virtually no one will give you a ten or even a nine. So, you don't want to let such an opportunity slip through your fingers. To make sure that it doesn't, you have to close with some persistence. Here is how I would start:

"I'm really happy to think that you think things went well because I am extremely interested in this opportunity because (state 2-3 substantive reasons.)"

"What, in your mind, makes me a good match for the position?'

Again, reinforce the positive comments with the use of Support Statements.

"Since you think that we have a good match here, we should move this to the next step, wouldn't you agree?" (Notice the tie-down question.)

If they respond with a 'yes,' close hard and get a commitment to whatever the next step would be. If they don't agree to move to the next step, uncover the objection, handle it and try closing again.

Response of 10

If by some fluke you get a ten response, you better close hard and immediately.

Conditional Closes

I'm going to give you one additional closing technique for those of you who want to get into the advanced placement class. This is a conditional close. It is sometimes referred to as a "just suppose" close because you are asking the interviewer to assume a hypothetical situation where a condition has been successfully met.

The time to use this close is when an interviewer throws a roadblock in front of your progress when you ask a closing question. Here is an example dialog:

You: "Would you feel comfortable bringing me onto your team?"

Interviewer: "I can't say until you have met my boss to get her approval."

You: "Obviously she needs to approve your choices, and I'm looking forward to meeting her. But may I ask you a hypothetical question? Just suppose that she does approve of me as a candidate, would you then start the offer process for me?"

This last question will put pressure on the interviewer and force them to reveal any other obstacles to your being hired. For example, the answer could come as follows:

Interviewer: "I'm not sure because I have two other candidates who are also finalists."

This example illustrates the power of the conditional close. If you had not tried it, you might not have heard about these other candidates and might have naively assumed you were going to get the job if you passed the final interview. You now know not to count on getting an offer even if you get past the final interview and that you should aggressively pursue other job leads.

12. Overcoming Language Barriers

If English Is Not Your First Language

Relocating to another country where the official language is different from your native one poses major challenges. Not the least of these is the cultural and linguistic adjustment that is required. I know this from personal experience because I was born in Hungary and English is not my mother tongue. Fortunately, I was only eight years old when I first started to learn English, so I was educated in English and grew up in the culture. As a result, my command of the language is indistinguishable from someone born in the US. My parents, on the other hand, learned English as adults and received no formal education in English. Because of this, whenever they opened their mouths to speak, it was obvious that they were immigrants.

Being foreign born and speaking with an accent is not, by itself, an obstacle to success in the US. You see proof of this every day on television as prominent people with foreign accents are interviewed. However, the following *will* hold a person back, including those who are US-born:

- Pronunciation that is difficult to understand. Poor enunciation is often worsened by rapid speech, especially during stressful situations like an interview.
- Lack of coherent expression of thought. This problem, too, can be exacerbated by nervousness and also by thinking in a foreign language and translating on the fly.
- Excessive grammatical errors. They can make it difficult for the listener to decode what is being said.
- Poor spelling in written communication.
- Misuse of words (malapropisms) in both written and oral communications.

If you are aware that you have any of the above problems, you can try the following strategies to overcome them:

1, Rehearse polished responses to frequently asked questions.

Nervousness can lead to rapid speech and more pronounced accents that can lead to a downward spiral in the interview. Knowing that there are certain questions that come up repeatedly in interviews, you can rehearse your responses ahead of time. Rehearsing will help you be less nervous in the interview. However, be careful. One problem with rehearsing a response too much is that you can sound like a robot. So, make sure that your answer sounds spontaneous. One effective way to do this is to write out your response as bullet points rather than as a word-for-word script. By using bullet points, each time you give the response you will deliver it slightly differently, and it will be less obvious that you have rehearsed.

2. Acknowledge your accent at the start of the interview.

After you have established rapport with the interviewer, but before you launch into the substance of the interview, you can say something like the following:

"I know that sometimes my accent can be difficult for people, especially when I am nervous in an interview. So, I would like to ask for your help. Could you please ask me to repeat any answers that are not completely clear to you? I don't want this interview to get off track because of any misunderstandings caused by my accent."

By saying something like the above, you have accomplished two things. First, you have given permission for the interviewer to address the matter of your accent. This will make it less likely that they will be embarrassed to ask you to repeat yourself. Second, by asking for their help, you have changed the dynamic in the relationship from the interviewer being on the opposite side of the conversation to being on your side to help you through the interview. This request for assistance is very powerful because it is encoded in our DNA to help others.

3. Control your anxiety.

The anxiety brought on by the stress of an interview can cause people to speak too quickly, rush their enunciation worsening their accent, jumble their words and become disorganized in expressing their thoughts. Even the most experienced interviewee will suffer from some level of nervousness. Be aware of the problem and find ways to control your anxiousness. What works best for me is thorough preparation and rehearsal.

4. Ask clarifying and confirming questions.

Before you answer a question, make sure that you have thoroughly understood it. So, ask any necessary clarifying questions, even if you need to do this a lot. Then, after you have delivered your response, ask a question to confirm that you answered the correct question, that the interviewer understood your answer and that it was on the mark.

These clarifications will slow down the flow of the interview, but accuracy of communication is more important than speed.

5. Use Active Listening.

Active Listening is another effective technique for ensuring that you and the interviewer are understanding each other.

6. Work to improve your English.

Here are some suggestions for long-term programs that will improve your English language skills:

- Read in English for pleasure, not just for work.
- Watch English-speaking movies, either subtitled in your native language or with closed captioning turned on.
- Take English language classes.
- Take classes in business writing. If a business writing class is unavailable, take a creative writing class.
- Use a website like www.grammarly.com to edit all your written work. The feedback from such editing will accelerate your learning and also keep you from perpetuating any errors. Be aware, however, that these sites use software that isn't infallible, and occasionally the corrections that they suggest may be wrong. So, consult people who write well before you accept every recommended change.

If the Interviewer Has the Language Problem

My recruiting practice was in the Silicon Valley/San Francisco Bay Area and focused on jobs in high tech. Since a high percentage of tech workers are foreign-born, it was very common to encounter an interviewer with a strong accent.

If you are ever interviewed by someone you find difficult to understand, you will face a dilemma. On the one hand, you don't want to possibly embarrass the interviewer by making it obvious that they have a language problem. On the other hand, you don't want to let their communication difficulties keep you from a job that you want. In this case, your need to succeed in the interview is more important than avoiding the potential embarrassment of the interviewer. Look at it this way, if they become embarrassed, they won't hire you, and you'll never see them again in any case. So, you have nothing to lose.

The way to handle a difficult-to-understand interviewer is to use Active Listening to repeat what you think you heard and then tag on a question to confirm that you understood the person. For example:

"I believe you said that you are planning on introducing advanced artificial intelligence software to help your customer service operations. Is that correct?

If you find yourself continuously asking clarifying questions that require the interviewer to repeat what they said, you may wish to acknowledge the fact in a diplomatic manner. You could say something along the following lines:

"Please accept my apologies for asking you to repeat yourself, but I am not that good at deciphering accents. So, I appreciate you taking the time to clarify what you said."

This is a very tactful way acknowledging the interviewer's accent problem and should not cause either of you discomfort. If handled in a polite way as above, most people will be fine with being asked to repeat things, but some may still take offense. Nevertheless, you have to risk upsetting the interviewer. If you and the interviewer are unable to communicate, you are not likely to get hired. So, you might as well face the situation head-on.

Even under the best of circumstances, humans are terrible communicators. They fail to clearly articulate what they mean, they filter or mishear what others say and don't always do enough to ensure that there are no misunderstandings. When you add language barriers to the mix, interviewing can become especially challenging. I hope I have given you some useful advice for dealing with the problem.

13. Informational Interviews

Informational interviews are appointments that you schedule to obtain various pieces of information to help you in your job search. Information collected during an informational interview might include industry or company intelligence, job search advice, target companies, referral names, hidden jobs, and more.

Prepare for an informational interview just as you would for a regular interview by defining your objectives and putting together your list of discovery questions.

The structure of the interview will be as follows:

1. *Establish Rapport* – Use the same approaches as for a regular interview.
2. *State Your Objectives and Agenda* – Same as for a regular interview except that the person is unlikely to have any objectives.
3. *Deliver Your Elevator Pitch* – This will be a two-minute summary of your background, skills, strengths, and accomplishments plus your goals for the future.
4. *Ask Questions* – Gather the information for which you came.
5. *Close* – In this case, you won't be asking for a job offer. Instead, ask for referrals and introductions. Get a commitment and time frames for any, if appropriate.
6. *Give Out Your Resume* – Don't hand out your resume until you have achieved your objectives. Otherwise, you will spend your time answering questions about your resume instead of getting answers to your questions.
7. *Leave* – Thank them and obtain permission to contact them with any additional questions.

Besides just taking information from them, you should consider what you can give back in return. Are there information, books, articles or introductions to your contacts that would be of interest to them? If you are meeting for a meal or coffee, pick up the tab.

14. Post-Interview Evaluation Form

Attached is a Post-Interview Evaluation form that you can use as a guide for self-assessment of each of your completed interviews. You may need more room to write than the form provides, so you should modify it as necessary. You may also wish to change it in other ways to suit your needs. It is intended only to be an initial guide for you.

Note: If you met several people on the same day, complete a separate form for each meeting.

Post-Interview Evaluation

Company: _____ Interviewer: _____ Date: _____

Length of Meeting: _____ Rate Your Performance (1-10): _____ Your Level of Interest (1-10): _____

Notes

What are the positives about the opportunity?

What are your concerns?

What were the challenging questions?

What did you do or say that went well?

What did you do or say that you would change in the future?

Which of your features did they receive well?

What were their concerns and how did you handle them?

What phase of the interview was easiest? Hardest?

Did you attempt to close? If not, why not? If yes, were you successful?

What are the next steps?

What follow-up is needed?

About the Author

Les Fenyves is a trainer and consultant on all matters related to looking for a job and to hiring. He teaches interviewing, resume-writing and job search skills to individuals, plus he advises startups on how to attract, select and retain key talent.

Les has an extensive background in both high-tech search and in sales and sales management. As the founder of James Moore and Associates (www.jamesmoore.com), the Silicon Valley's longest-established search firm, he was its Managing Director and also a senior recruiter for over thirty years until his retirement in 2018. Previously he held positions of Branch Manager and Regional Vice President at, what was then, the largest international search firm dedicated to the computer field. Early in his career, he worked in technical and sales positions in the computer industry.

In addition to personally helping thousands of professionals to improve their careers, Les has hired and trained dozens of successful sales professionals. He has culled his personal experience plus those of his associates for the advice contained in this guide.

Made in the USA
Coppell, TX
08 September 2020